My revision notes

OCR AS/A-level History

BRITAIN
1930–1997

Mike Wells

Series editor
Nicholas Fellows

HODDER
EDUCATION
AN HACHETTE UK COMPANY

Acknowledgements

The Publishers would like to thank the following for permission to reproduce copyright material. Text credits: **p.23** *br*, **p.27** *r*, **p.29** *l*, **p.44** *br*. Reproduced with permission of Curtis Brown, London on behalf of The Estate of Winston S. Churchill. © The Estate of Winston S. Churchill.

Every effort has been made to trace all copyright holders, but if any have been inadvertently overlooked, the Publishers will be pleased to make the necessary arrangements at the first opportunity.

Although every effort has been made to ensure that website addresses are correct at the time of going to press, Hodder Education cannot be held responsible for the content of any website mentioned in this book. It is sometimes possible to find a relocated web page by typing in the address of the home page for a website in the URL window of your browser.

Hachette UK's policy is to use papers that are natural, renewable and recyclable products and made from wood grown in well-managed forests and other controlled sources. The logging and manufacturing processes are expected to conform to the environmental regulations of the country of origin.

Orders: please contact Bookpoint Ltd, 130 Milton Park, Abingdon, Oxon OX14 4SE. Telephone: +44 (0)1235 827720. Fax: +44 (0)1235 400454. Email education@ bookpoint.co.uk Lines are open from 9 a.m. to 5 p.m., Monday to Saturday, with a 24-hour message answering service. You can also order through our website: www.hoddereducation.co.uk

ISBN: 978 1 4718 7594 6

© Mike Wells 2017

First published in 2017 by

Hodder Education,
An Hachette UK Company
Carmelite House
50 Victoria Embankment
London EC4Y 0DZ

www.hoddereducation.co.uk

Impression number   10 9 8 7 6

Year   2022

Cover photo © Courtesy of the Library of Congress, LC-USW33-019093
Illustrations by Integra
Typeset by Integra Software Services Pvt. Ltd., Pondicherry, India
Printed and bound by CPI Group (UK) Ltd, Croydon, CR0 4YY

A catalogue record for this title is available from the British Library.

My Revision Planner

REVISED

4

Introduction

Unit 1: British period study and enquiry

Unit 1 involves the study of a period of British history. At both A- and AS-level there are two sections to the examination. Section A is the enquiry section and Section B is the essay section. In the enquiry section there will be four primary written sources and one question for the A-level examination, and three primary written sources and two questions for the AS-level examination. Section B will consist of two essays, of which you will have to answer one. The type of essay set for both the AS and A-level examinations are similar, but the AS mark scheme does not have a Level 6 (see page 7).

Britain, 1930–97

The specification lists the content of the period study element, which is Britain, 1951–97, under four key topics.
- Key topic 1 – Conservative domination, 1951–64
- Key topic 2 – Labour and Conservative Governments, 1964–79
- Key topic 3 – Thatcher and the end of consensus, 1979–97
- Key topic 4 – Britain's position in the world, 1951–97

The specification lists the content of the enquiry element, which is Churchill 1929–51 under three key topics.
- Key topic 1 – Churchill's view of events, 1929–40
- Key topic 2 – Churchill as wartime Prime Minister
- Key topic 3 – Churchill and international diplomacy, 1939–51

Although each period of study is set out in chronological sections in the specification, an exam question may arise from one or more of these sections.

AS-level

The AS examination which you may be taking includes all the content.

You are required to answer:
- Section A: two questions. They are source-based questions and will require you to use your knowledge to explain, analyse and evaluate three primary sources. The first question will require you to consider the utility of one of the sources for a particular issue and is worth 10 marks. The second question will require you to explain, analyse and evaluate the three sources in relation to an issue and is worth 20 marks. The section is worth 30 marks.

- Section B: one essay question from a choice of two. The essays require you to explain, analyse and assess an issue, using your knowledge to reach a balanced judgement about the question. The question is worth 20 marks.

The exam lasts one and a half hours, and you are advised to spend slightly more time on Section A.

At AS-level, Unit 2 will be worth a total of 50 marks and 50 per cent of the AS-level examination.

A-level

The A-level examination at the end of the course includes all the content.

You are required to answer ONE question from Section A and one essay from Section B from a choice of TWO questions.
- Section A is the enquiry question and will contain four written primary sources. You will be asked to use the four sources to test a hypothesis by considering the provenance and content of the sources and applying your own knowledge to the sources to reach a judgement about them in relation to the issue in the question. This is the same as AS question 2 but uses four sources instead of three.
- The essay questions are similar in style and requirement to the AS essay question, except that in order to reach the highest level you will need to show a more developed sense of judgement.

The exam lasts for one and a half hours. You should spend slightly longer on Section A than B.

At A-level, Unit 1 will be worth a total of 50 marks and 25 per cent of the A-level.

In both the AS and A-level examinations you are being tested on your ability to:
- use relevant historical information
- the skill of analysing factors and reaching a judgement.

How to use this book

This book has been designed to help you develop the knowledge and skills necessary to succeed in the examination.

● The book is divided into four sections – one for each section of the AS and A-level specifications.
● Each section is made up of a series of topics organised into double-page spreads.
● On the left-hand page you will find a summary of the key content you will need to learn.
● Words in bold in the key content are defined in the glossary (see pages 98–99).
● On the right-hand page you will find exam-focused activities.

Together these two strands of the book will provide you with the knowledge and skills essential for examination success.

▼ **Key historical content**

▼ **Exam-focused activities**

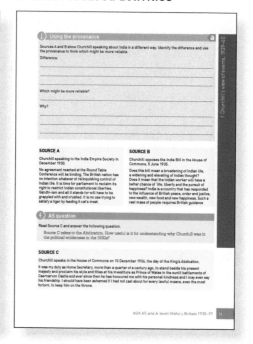

Examination activities

There are three levels of exam-focused activities:

● Band 1 activities are designed to develop the foundation skills needed to pass the exam. These have a green heading and this symbol:
● Band 2 activities are designed to build on the skills developed in Band 1 activities and to help you to achieve a C grade. These have an orange heading and this symbol:
● Band 3 activities are designed to enable you to access the highest grades. These have a purple heading and this symbol:

Some of the activities have answers or suggested answers on pages 102–104. These have the following symbol to indicate this:

Each section ends with exam-style questions and sample answers with commentary. This will give you guidance on what is expected to achieve the top grade.

You can also keep track of your revision by ticking off each topic heading in the book, or by ticking the checklist on the contents page. Tick each box when you have:

● revised and understood a topic
● completed the activities.

Mark schemes

For some of the activities in the book it will be useful to refer to the mark schemes for this paper. Below are abbreviated forms.

AS-level

Level	Question 1 Utility	Question 2 All 3 sources	Question 3 or 4 Essay
5	Good focus, evaluation using provenance and context to engage with the issue to reach an analysis of its utility. (9–10)	Good focus, sources are evaluated using provenance and context, although there may be some imbalance, to reach an analysis of the issue. (17–20)	Mostly focused, supported answer with good analysis and evaluation to reach a supported judgement. (17–20)
4	Mostly focused, evaluated using provenance and context, with some imbalance to engage with the issue to reach an analysis of its utility. (7–8)	Mostly focused, sources are evaluated using some provenance and context to reach an analysis of the issue. (13–16)	Some focus with support, analysis with limited evaluation and judgement. (13–16)
3	Partial focus and evaluation of either context or provenance to produce a partial analysis of its utility. (5–6)	Partial focus and evaluation, some context to produce a partial analysis of the issue. (9–12)	Partial focus on the question, with some knowledge and analysis, but little or no judgement. (9–12)
2	Limited focus, general or stock evaluation to produce a limited analysis of the issue. (3–4)	Limited focus, evaluation is general as is context. General analysis of the issue. (5–8)	Focus is descriptive and may be more on the topic than the question. Any analysis may be implied. (5–8)
1	Answer is on the topic, basic evaluation and general knowledge. Simple or general analysis of the issue. (1–2)	Answer is on the topic, basic evaluation, much description of the sources and general contextual knowledge leading to a simple analysis of the issue. (1–4)	Focus on the topic and attempts at analysis will be little more than assertion. (1–4)

A-level

Level	Question	Essay
6	Well focused, sources are fully evaluated using provenance and context to reach a fully supported analysis of the issue. (26–30)	Well-focused, supported answer with very good analysis and developed evaluation to reach a supported and sustained judgement. (17–20)
5	Good focus, sources are evaluated using provenance and context, although there may be some imbalance, to reach an analysis of the issue. (21–25)	Mostly focused, supported answer with good analysis and evaluation to reach a supported judgement. (13–16)
4	Mostly focused, sources are evaluated using some provenance and context to reach an analysis of the issue. (16–20)	Some focus with support, analysis with limited evaluation and judgement. (10–12)
3	Partial focus and evaluation, some context to produce a partial analysis of the issue. (11–15)	Partial focus on the question, with some knowledge and analysis, but little or no judgement. (7–9)
2	Limited focus, evaluation is general as is context. General analysis of the issue. (6–10)	Focus is descriptive and may be more on the topic than the question. Any analysis may be implied. (4–6)
1	Answer is on the topic, basic evaluation, much description of the sources and general contextual knowledge leading to a simple analysis of the issue.(1–5)	Focus on the topic and attempts at analysis will be little more than assertion. (1–3)

1 Churchill's view of events, 1929–40

Why was Churchill out of office in 1929–39?

Winston Churchill was a highly experienced minister and one of Britain's leading politicians, but during a vital period he was out of office. The Conservatives lost the general election of May 1929, and when Macdonald formed his **National Government** in August 1931 Churchill was not invited to be part of it. When the National Government became increasingly Conservative in nature, Churchill was still 'in the wilderness', and it was not until the start of the war in 1939 that he was back in the cabinet.

Previous reputation

Churchill was not liked by either Labour or the Liberals so would have been a difficult person to have in a coalition in 1931. There were several reasons for this:

- Labour remembered his bitter attacks on trade unions during the **General Strike** of 1926 and even his use of troops against strikers in South Wales before the First World War.
- His responsibility for the failed Gallipoli attacks in 1915 also made him unpopular.
- He was blamed for high unemployment because of his policy of returning Britain to the **Gold Standard** in 1925, which raised export prices.
- He had taken a strong line against making concessions to Indian self-government, which went against the views of moderates in all parties.
- He had been critical not only of Labour policy on India between 1929 and 1931 but also of the Conservative leader Baldwin's support for negotiation with Indian nationalists and Gandhi.
- He was considered to have aligned himself with extreme right-wing imperialists and to be out of touch with more modern Conservative policies.

Churchill's stance in the mid-1930s

Churchill was not invited back into government in the mid-1930s when Stanley Baldwin, and later **Neville Chamberlain**, became Prime Ministers and the former Labour Prime Minister MacDonald retired. The reasons for this centred around his speaking out on the danger posed by Germany and his belief that Britain should rearm generally and needed greater air defences in particular. This was out of line with mainstream thinking. He seemed too willing to risk war again when public opinion was opposed to conflict, and there was a belief in reaching negotiated settlements. Chamberlain became Prime Minister in 1937 and was very committed to a policy of **Appeasement**. Churchill's speeches made better relations with Germany more difficult (see page 14 for more on Appeasement), and he did not seem to offer a realistic alternative to the Government's policy.

Churchill's criticism of British defences seemed hypocritical because it was his defence cuts of the 1920s which laid the basis for Britain's military weakness. The urge to rearm also seemed to ignore the economic realities of the 1930s, when government spending had been cut and unemployment was high. Spending money on what might be seen as an 'arms race' when there were very stringent conditions on any help for Britain's unemployed was very difficult to justify. Alongside this, his outspoken support for Edward VIII during the Abdication crisis put him outside the consensus of his own party and Britain's establishment (see page 10 for more on the Abdication).

Churchill's style

Aside from his policies, Churchill's style seemed out of touch. His way of speaking seemed old fashioned and contrasted with that of both Baldwin and Chamberlain, who had a more modern way of speaking to the electorate. He also did not have a strong following in the Conservative Party and surrounded himself with other 'outsiders'.

Mind map

Make a copy of the mind map below and use the information on the opposite page to show how each issue explains why Churchill was not in office.

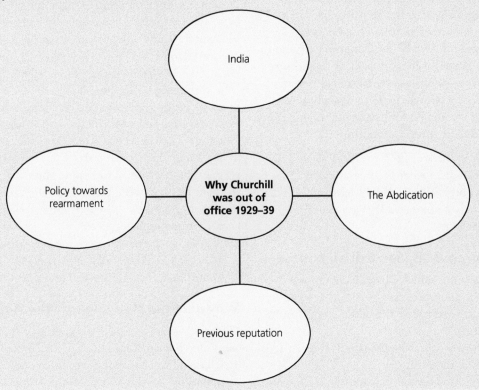

India

Policy towards rearmament

Why Churchill was out of office 1929–39

The Abdication

Previous reputation

Spot the inference **a**

High-level answers avoid just summarising or paraphrasing the sources, and instead make inferences from the sources. Below are a source and a series of statements. Read Source A and decide which of the statements

- make an inference from the source (I)
- paraphrase the source (P)
- summarise the source (S)
- cannot be justified from the source (X).

	Statement	I	P	S	X
1	The Labour party hated Churchill.				
2	Even though he was admired for some personal qualities, Churchill was not seen as solid and trustworthy and this made it difficult for him to be in office.				
3	Churchill was very talented and charming but he loved crises, his judgement was faulty and he liked to make things happen.				
4	Churchill was obviously the most talented of the politicians and he was charming and had very good manners. This did not prevent some people thinking that he was dangerous and loved crises.				

SOURCE A

Arthur Ponsonby, a Labour MP who was formally a Liberal, explains his view of Churchill in a letter from March 1930. Quoted from R.R. James, Churchill, A Study in Failure.

He [Churchill] is so far and away the most talented man in political life and he is also charming and a gentleman, but this does not prevent me from feeling politically that he is a great danger, largely because of his love of crisis and his faulty judgement. He once said to me 'I like things to happen, and if they don't happen, I like to make them happen.'

India and the Abdication

What were the problems in India?

In India there were widespread calls for independence from Britain, especially after British troops had fired on a crowd in the Amritsar Massacre of 1919. Growing nationalist agitation was led by the Congress Party, and a non-violent but powerful civil disobedience campaign was led by Gandhi. Reliance on repression to govern India gave Britain a poor international reputation and risked alienating the support for British rule among many of the richer and more privileged Indians.

The British Government made conciliatory moves. In 1930 and 1931 Gandhi attended talks in London. This was followed by the passing of the Government of India Act in 1935 which set up elected legislatures and increased the electorate.

Why did Churchill oppose British policy?

Churchill opposed the British Government's moves towards change in India because:
- he loved the Raj and had served in the army in India as a young man
- he objected to any concessions to popular protest and threats to lawful authority
- he thought that Gandhi and Indian nationalism would be content only with full independence, so concessions were a waste of time
- he thought that independence would lead to disastrous conflicts between Muslims and Hindus and put power in the hands of India's most powerful caste – the Brahmins
- he believed in the superiority of the white race and its destiny to rule
- he saw British power in Europe and the world as dependent on its continuing control of its Empire.

What were the consequences?

Even some of Churchill's friends and supporters found some of his views on India too extreme. He had aligned himself with extreme and old-fashioned imperialists, and cut himself off from mainstream Conservative Party opinion. This alienated Prime Ministers Baldwin and Chamberlain, who did not trust him to be in government.

The Abdication

A stable monarchy was important as it helped Britain's reputation abroad and the monarchy had been a vital element in encouraging patriotism and sacrifice during the First World War. When Edward VIII succeeded to the throne in 1936 he wanted to marry Mrs Simpson. This threatened stability because:
- marrying an American who had been twice divorced would have been difficult for the British public to accept at a time when divorce still bore a stigma
- the Archbishop of Canterbury was concerned about marrying a divorced woman in church
- there may have been problems in the Empire in accepting a marriage in which she was simply the royal consort rather than Queen
- the cabinet did not give its approval for the marriage and therefore if Edward had married Mrs Simpson, the Government would have had to resign.

Why did Churchill support the King?

Churchill joined the small group of 'King's friends' and supported Edward because:
- Churchill had a sincere devotion to hereditary monarchy, and saw it as his duty to support the rightful King
- he spoke of his friendship with the King when he had been Prince of Wales
- he possibly was unsympathetic to those 'respectable' members of the establishment who seemed to be opposed to the King finding happiness
- he was an emotional person and was moved by the royal love story.

What were the consequences?

As with India, Churchill was in a minority and at odds with his party and its leadership. He seemed oblivious to public opinion and appeared eccentric and old-fashioned.

! Using the provenance

a

Sources A and B show Churchill speaking about India in a different way. Identify the difference and use the provenance to think which might be more reliable.

Difference:

_____

_____

_____

Which might be more reliable?

_____

Why?

_____

_____

_____

_____

SOURCE A

Churchill speaking to the India Empire Society in December 1930.

No agreement reached at the Round Table Conference will be binding. The British nation has no intention whatever of relinquishing control of Indian life. It is time for parliament to reclaim its right to restrict Indian constitutional liberties. Gandhi-ism and all it stands for will have to be grappled with and crushed. It is no use trying to satisfy a tiger by feeding it cat's meat.

SOURCE B

Churchill opposes the India Bill in the House of Commons, 5 June 1935.

Does this bill mean a broadening of Indian life, a widening and elevating of Indian thought? Does it mean that the Indian worker will have a better chance of 'life, liberty and the pursuit of happiness'? India is a country that has responded to the influence of British peace, order and justice, new wealth, new food and new happiness. Such a vast mass of people requires British guidance.

↓ AS question

Read Source C and answer the following question.

> Source C refers to the Abdication. How useful is it for understanding why Churchill was in the political wilderness in the 1930s?

SOURCE C

Churchill speaks in the House of Commons on 10 December 1936, the day of the King's Abdication.

It was my duty as Home Secretary, more than a quarter of a century ago, to stand beside his present majesty and proclaim his style and titles at his investiture as Prince of Wales in the sunlit battlements of Caernarvon Castle and ever since then he has honoured me with his personal kindness and I may even say his friendship. I should have been ashamed if I had not cast about for every lawful means, even the most forlorn, to keep him on the throne.

Churchill's attitude to Germany after 1933

Churchill saw the Hitler regime that was established in 1933 as dangerous. He saw continuity with the situation before 1914, when Germany had been a threat to world peace. Churchill's historical knowledge and writings also influenced his outlook. He had made an influential study of the origins of the First World War in his book *The World Crisis* which stressed the rise of Germany and its impact on the balance of power in Europe and the threat of German expansion. Now it appeared that Germany was once more seeking to overturn the balance of power established in 1919. He was also influenced by a multi-volume historical account of his ancestor, John Churchill, the Duke of Marlborough, in whose palace at Blenheim Churchill had been born. In *Marlborough, His Life and Times*, Churchill had portrayed England fighting against the domination of Europe by the powerful and absolutist king Louis XIV and being defeated by the military skill of England's general, Churchill. It was the fear of the domination of the continent by a single power that had driven British policy over the centuries and Churchill's historical interests led him to think that this was happening once again with Hitler's Germany.

Churchill had been part of the government which had established the peace treaty with Germany in 1919 and was worried that the new ultra-nationalist regime would break it. He feared that a powerful Germany would upset the balance of power in Europe and take advantage of weaker states established after the First World War in eastern Europe. He was also concerned about the violent behaviour of the Nazis and disliked the Nazi party's anti-Semitism. However, Churchill did not oppose dictatorship in itself, and had been sympathetic to Mussolini's rule in Italy.

What was his attitude to developments in Germany?

Churchill repeatedly voiced his concerns about developments in Germany. He saw German **rearmament** as a threat, and as early as 1934 he warned against Germany developing stronger air power than Britain. When Hitler reintroduced conscription in 1935, Churchill was worried this was another sign of a revival of German militarism. The British Government's response to German rearmament was to try to limit it through the Anglo-German Naval Treaty of 1935. Churchill criticised this as a sign of weakness. He also thought that it was short-sighted of Britain to fall out with Mussolini, hitherto an opponent of Hitler, over the Italian invasion of Ethiopia.

Why did Churchill not gain more support for his views?

There were many reasons why Churchill's attitude to Germany was unpopular in Britain.

- Some thought Germany had been treated too harshly by the Treaty of Versailles.
- There was a great deal of anti-war feeling and rearmament was unpopular.
- Churchill seemed to be advocating initiating another arms race. It was widely thought that the naval race between Britain and Germany had led to the First World War. He also appeared somewhat hypocritical since he had initiated much British **disarmament** in the 1920s.
- Some in Germany and those on the political right in Britain sympathised with Hitler due to his opposition to communism and the national revival he had initiated in Germany, thus even Churchill's natural allies did not support his views.
- Churchill's worry about German air power so early seemed to be too alarmist.
- Churchill seemed to be putting possible clashes with Germany ahead of Britain's need to look after her own people at a time of economic distress.
- Given Churchill's views on the Empire and India, his anti-German stance seemed to be yet another example of his living in the past and harking back to Edwardian England, which had viewed Germany as the main enemy.
- Churchill seemed to ignore the role of the League of Nations in keeping peace at a time when there were still high hopes for the League's success.

Support or challenge?

Below are an exam-style question that asks you to agree with a specific statement and a series of sources relevant to the question. Use your own knowledge and the information on the opposite page to decide whether the sources support or challenge the statement in the question and explain why in the boxes.

Using these three sources in their historical context, assess how far they support the view that Churchill's failure to get more support for his views on Germany and rearmament was his own fault.

Source	Support	Challenge
A		
B		
C		

SOURCE A

Baldwin speaks in the House of Commons about the public support for rearmament, 12 November 1936.

There was probably a stronger pacifist feeling running through the country at any time since the War. You will remember the election in Fulham in 1933. I asked myself what chance there was within the next two or three years of public feeling being changed enough to give the government support for rearmament?

SOURCE B

Churchill speaks about Germany in a radio broadcast in November 1934. Quoted from R.R. James, Churchill, A Study in Failure.

Only a few hours away by air there dwells a nation of nearly 70 million who are being taught from childhood to think of war and conquest as a great and glorious exercise and death in battle as the noblest fate of man. It is in the grip of ruthless men preaching a doctrine of racial pride. We must without another hour's delay begin to make ourselves the strongest air power in the European world.

SOURCE C

Lord Halifax, then a member of the Government as Lord Privy Seal and later to be Foreign Secretary, gives his view on the threat of war in a speech to the House of Commons in 1935.

Are we to judge the situation so serious that everything has to give way to military reconditioning of our Defence forces? Such a conclusion seems to rest on the view that war is inevitable, that there is a certainty as to the early imminence of war which I am not prepared to accept.

 Doing reliability well **a**

Below are an exam-style question and a set of definitions listing common reasons why sources can be unreliable. Using Sources A–C above, for each source write a critical account of whether it is a reliable or unreliable piece of evidence, justifying your answer by referring to the definitions below.

Using these three sources in their historical context, assess how far they support the view that Churchill's failure to get more support for his views on Germany and rearmament was his own fault.

- Vested interest: the source is written so that the writer can protect his own power or interests.
- Second-hand report: the writer is not in a position to know and is relying on someone else's information.
- Expertise: the source is written on a subject on which the author is an expert.
- Political bias: the source is written by a politician and it reflected their political views.
- Reputation: the source is written to protect the writer's reputation.

Churchill and Appeasement

From 1937 the policy of Appeasement was pursued by Neville Chamberlain. The key element of the policy was the Munich Agreement of 1938 in which Chamberlain agreed to the dismembering of the independent state of Czechoslovakia, making the German-speaking part, the Sudetenland, part of Germany and allowing Slovakia to be separate from a reduced Czech state. Britain had accepted Hitler's annexation of Austria (the so-called *Anschluss* in 1938) but the Munich Conference accepted Germany taking over the territory of people who were not Germans.

Churchill's reaction to Appeasement

Churchill was highly critical of the Munich Agreement. As Chamberlain had given in to German demands in a conference on German soil, Churchill believed Britain had come across as weak and was in danger of being dominated by Germany. In his opinion, the Munich Agreement strengthened Germany and would make it more difficult for Britain to control future expansion. According to Churchill, the agreement was not a negotiated settlement, but 'a defeat without a war'. It was a moral defeat, not only in being instrumental in the break up of an independent state, but also in Britain's 'moral health' in failing to maintain a stand against Hitler after he had gone back on his word.

What was Churchill's policy?

With hindsight, Churchill's views of Appeasement appear correct, but his criticism of the Munich Agreement and his view that Britain should have gone to war in 1938 seemed quite unrealistic at the time. Many people in Britain thought that Czechoslovakia was simply 'a far away country' about which they knew nothing. In any case, rearmament had not really begun, and there was no expeditionary force ready to send to Europe. It was also far from certain that Britain would find allies in a war against Germany. There was no certainty that France would have supported joint military action, even though the French had an alliance with both the USSR and the Czechs. Military chiefs in Britain doubted the real strength of Russia as an ally, given the purges of military leaders being carried out there. In addition, the dominions in the Commonwealth could not be relied on, and there was little possibility of the USA joining Britain in the event of war.

Churchill believed that a strong stand by Britain and other nations would deter Germany and would prevent the balance of power shifting in central Europe towards a powerful German state. He may have also believed that a strong stand would have encouraged opposition to Hitler within Germany itself.

Why was it criticised at the time?

Churchill's alternative to Appeasement was criticised by many in Britain. As well as the uncertainty that other countries would join with Britain, the British chiefs of staff were worried that war against Germany would also become a war against Hitler's allies, Italy and Japan. Churchill did not really speak or write much about Japan and neglected its possible threat to Britain's Asian colonies in the event of war. There was also little evidence that German generals or many German people would turn against a generally popular Nazi regime.

However, Churchill's opposition had some merit:

- The breaking of the Munich Agreement by Hitler when he occupied the Czech state made Britain look weak and confirmed Churchill's suspicions of Hitler's expansionist agenda.
- Though Munich gave Britain a chance to rearm. Germany also rearmed at considerable speed from 1938–39.
- In 1938, there was the chance of working with France and the USSR and also of having 35 divisions of Czech troops fighting on interior lines of defence.
- The Germans might well have found it difficult to conquer Czechoslovakia as they would have to have kept forces on other fronts to meet a possible allied attack.

Linking sources

Below are a question and four sources. In one colour draw links between the sources to show ways in which they show that Churchill was being realistic about Germany, and in another colour draw links between the courses to show ways in which they disagree.

Read Sources A–D How far do they show that Churchill was being realistic about Appeasement?

SOURCE A

Churchill speaks in the House of Commons on the Munich Agreement in October 1938.

We have sustained a defeat without a war. This is only the beginning of the reckoning. This is only the first sip of a bitter cup which will be proffered to us year by year.

SOURCE B

Chamberlain writes to his sister on 20 March 1938. Adapted from Nigel Knight, Churchill. The Greatest Briton Unmasked.

The plan of the Grand Alliance, as Winston calls it, has everything to be said for it until you come to its practicalities. You only have to look at the map to see that nothing that France or Britain could do could possibly save Czechoslovakia.

SOURCE C

Churchill speaks of joint action to prevent German aggression in the House of Commons on 14 March 1938.

If a number of states were assembled round Great Britain and France in a solemn treaty for mutual alliance against aggression: if they had their forces marshalled in what you might call a Grand Alliance; if they had their military arrangements concerted... then I say you might arrest this approaching war.

SOURCE D

The memoirs of a leading military figure recall the situation in 1938. From Lord Ismay, The Memoirs of General Lord Ismay.

When one remembers the almost hysterical reception accorded to Chamberlain on his return from Munich and the flood of congratulatory messages from all sorts and conditions of men the world over, it is very doubtful if we had fought at the time of Munich whether we should have done so as a united nation. It is even more doubtful whether we would have done so as a united Commonwealth and Empire.

Add your own knowledge

Annotate Sources A–D with your own knowledge to add evidence which either supports or challenges the view presented in each source about whether Churchill was realistic in his view of Appeasement.

Why Churchill became Prime Minister in 1940

Churchill became Prime Minister on 10 May 1940. This was a historic appointment but he was not generally popular within the Conservative Party or with the military chiefs or the King and Queen.

- His attacks on the Government in the 1930s had made him enemies within the Conservative Party.
- Chamberlain was a very well respected leader.
- Churchill had been overbearing as a member of the war cabinet as First Lord of the Admiralty.
- He had urged the mining of Norwegian waters which had provoked the **Norway Campaign**, which had failed.
- The naval commanders found him interfering and overbearing.
- Many civil servants found the prospect of Churchill in power to be worrying.
- He had quite a record of failures – Gallipoli in the First World War and the restoration of the Gold Standard in 1926.
- He had been out of office for most of the 1930s and was in his 60s.
- The Queen resented his support for Edward VIII, and both she and George VI had admired Chamberlain and supported Appeasement.
- His supporters were on the fringes of Conservative politics and were not appointed to high office when he became Prime Minister.

Reasons for Chamberlain's resignation

It was difficult for Chamberlain as 'a man of peace' to become a war leader, and by May 1940 there was a feeling in parliament (among Conservatives as well as Labour MPs) that he was not waging war well enough. Britain had not done well in the fighting in Norway against Germany, and there had been no attempt to engage with German forces in the west. Wavering support for Chamberlain was shown in the debate in the House of Commons over Norway, when 40 Conservative MPs had voted against the Government and a further 40 abstained. There were some bitter words from the Conservative MP Leo Amery, quoting Cromwell dismissing the Rump Parliament, 'You have sat long enough for any good you have been doing. Depart, I say and let us have done with you. In the name of God, go.'

As Chamberlain was seriously ill by this time, it was probably accepted by many MPs that a change was needed.

Reasons for Churchill's appointment

Churchill had considerable popular support in the country due to his stand against Appeasement and for his obvious determination to pursue war vigorously. He had the support of a group of Conservative MPs, and Labour backed him also. However, Lord Halifax was the preferred candidate of most Conservatives and was a friend of the King. There were problems with Halifax becoming Prime Minister, though. He was associated with the policy of Appeasement and, as a peer, he could not sit in the House of Commons. Most importantly, he made it clear that he would not accept the post. That left Churchill as the only possible person who could gain the support of most MPs.

Despite his misgivings, the King appointed Churchill as Prime Minister. Churchill brought many qualities to the role:

- He was a powerful orator.
- His newspaper articles were widely read.
- He was a very experienced minister.
- He had a sense of destiny and entitlement.
- He was seen as a highly individual and determined leader who would invigorate the war effort.

Perhaps most importantly, the German invasion of The Netherlands and Belgium prior to invading France created a sense of urgency and indicated that Britain needed a leader who understood war.

Support or challenge?

Below is an exam question which asks you about a specific statement. Look at Sources A–D and decide whether the sources support or challenge the view. Fill in the boxes in the table below showing what statements in the source support or challenge the view. This is the first stage in answering the question and will not by itself gain high marks.

Using these four sources in their historical context assess how far they support the view that Churchill was appointed Prime Minister in 1940 because it was thought that he was the best man for the job.

Source	Support	Challenge
A		
B		
C		
D		

SOURCE A

A political admirer of Churchill recalls the position in 1940. From Duff Cooper, Old Men Forget.

The choice lay between Churchill and Lord Halifax. Churchill's reputation had risen sharply since 1939. He had shown himself a highly competent First lord of the Admiralty. His speeches in the Commons had been better than any of his colleagues. Everything he had prophesied in the past had come true ... The choice was obvious.

SOURCE B

From the diaries of Chamberlain's Private Secretary who would go on to work closely with Churchill. Sir John Colville, The Fringes of Power: Downing Street Diaries, 1939–1955.

The King disliked the change to Churchill and would have preferred Halifax. The feeling in the Conservative party was represented by a letter from Queen Mary to my mother, hoping that I would not go on to work with Mr Churchill. Yet Winston is a popular hero and so much the war leader that he cannot be dropped.

SOURCE C

From the diary of Leo Kennedy, the diplomatic editor of The Times, 4 May 1940.

What is needed is that Winston should take a rest. He is overdoing himself and taking the strain by stoking out with Champagne, liqueurs etc. He has got into the habit of calling conferences and subordinates after one a.m., which naturally upsets the admirals, so there is a general atmosphere of strain at the Admiralty, which is all wrong.

SOURCE D

Churchill recalls the position in May 1940. From Winston Churchill, The Gathering Storm.

Failure at Trondheim! Stalemate at Narvik! Considering the prominent part I played in these events (in the Norway campaign) it was a miracle that I survived and maintained my position in public esteem and Parliamentary confidence.

 Add your own knowledge

Annotate sources A–D with your own knowledge to add evidence that either supports or challenges the views presented in each source about whether Churchill was appointed Prime Minister because he was thought to be the best man for the job.

Exam focus

Below is an AS exam-style question. Read the source, question, model response and the comments on the answer.

Use your knowledge of the international situation in the 1930s to assess how useful Source A is as evidence for how realistic Churchill's view of British foreign policy was.

SOURCE A

Churchill speaks about what Britain should do following the Anschluss with Austria, in a speech in the House of Commons, 14 March 1938.

The gravity of the event of March 12 cannot be exaggerated. Europe is confronted with a programme of aggression, unfolding stage by stage, and there is only one course open, not only to us but to other countries, either to submit like Austria or else to take effective measures. If we go on waiting on events, how much shall we throw away of resources now available for our security and the maintenance of peace. How many of our friends will be alienated; how many potential allies shall we see go one by one down the grisly gulf. How many times will bluff succeed?

The source is useful in showing both how unrealistic Churchill was in looking at the international situation, yet how realistic he was about the likely future actions of Hitler. He was speaking in the Commons to urge more decisive action, so he may have exaggerated the possibilities in frustration about Baldwin's foreign policy of drift. Churchill was well known for his warnings about German aggression and for his fears that Germany was building up its armed forces and its air force and would be a threat to Europe again. These developments did allow Hitler to become a threat. He speaks of the government 'waiting on events' because he had been urging rearmament and greater preparations and also more effort to get alliances with other countries, which Baldwin had not effectively done.

However, the Anschluss was indeed a grave event and subsequent events did show that, even if it was not part of a 'programme' of aggression, it did lead to more aggression by Hitler in gaining the Sudentenland from Czechoslovakia and then dismembering the country in March 1939 and taking Bohemia and Moravia. So this was realistic of Churchill and indeed Chamberlain agreed, though his idea of 'effective action' was different from Churchill's. This is because Britain did not have great resources available. In March 1938 there was no expeditionary force ready; the army was spread round the Empire and the great programme of air defence was not fully under way. The navy alone could not have helped prevent German expansion in Europe, also, it is difficult to see which 'friends' Churchill meant. France was unwilling to commit to action and relied on her defences; the USSR was not a friend and was in any case in the grip of major upheaval over the purges; and the USA was deeply isolationist. No major power would be alienated by lack of action and the 'friends' in the Empire were against intervention in European affairs, especially since Austria was a German-speaking country and there was a history of both Germany and Austria being united. Churchill was to repeat the theme of 'potential allies' but this was not realistic analysis but merely a hope. The countries of eastern Europe were not strong enough – or in the case of Poland – willing to be allies. It was unlikely that the USSR would be an ally and Churchill had been opposed to Communism.

The speech is typical of many of Churchill's utterances warning against German expansion but not offering anything very realistic to prevent it, especially given the reluctance of both British public opinion and opinion in the Empire to take 'effective action'.

This shows a good focus on the question of 'realistic' and makes a good distinction.

This explains why Churchill was speaking.

Though more might have been said about Baldwin, there is knowledge of the context of the Anschluss.

There is a lot of good support for a critique of Churchill's point about friends supporting the view that he was not being realistic.

This is a strong, high level response. The answer uses contextual knowledge to assess the realism of the speech and to suggest what it is useful for showing. There is reference to the provenance and the situation which led to Churchill expressing his views. The answer demonstrates understanding of the source and links it to the question. There is also use of sound contextual knowledge and good awareness of the nature of the evidence.

What makes a good answer?

Make a list of the characteristics that make a good answer. Use the example and comments to help you.

Activity

Look at this question and Source B and write an answer which has similar qualities to the example on the opposite page.
Use your own knowledge of the international situation of the 1930s to assess how useful source B is for evidence for how realistic Churchill's view of British foreign policy was

SOURCE B

W.S. Churchill, The Gathering Storm, *1948*

Had we acted with reasonable prudence and healthy energy war might never have come to pass. Based on superior air power Britain and France could have safely invoked the aid of the League of Nations and all the states of Europe would have gathered behind them.

2 Churchill as wartime Prime Minister

Churchill's stance in 1940 and his style of leadership

As soon as Winston Churchill became Prime Minister the war took a more dangerous turn, as German forces made rapid advances in a **Blitzkrieg** attack through the Low Countries and into France. By 28 May, British forces were cut off from the French, and there was a danger they would be destroyed at Dunkirk. It also looked likely that Italy would join the war against Britain. Alongside this, Britain's gold reserves were running out, and there was a danger that obtaining war supplies from North America would not be possible.

What was Churchill's stance?

Churchill's reaction to these events was ultimately very important for the Allied victory. He was completely focused and totally determined that the single aim of the war was victory and that Britain's survival and that of the Empire would be impossible without focusing on this single aim. In defiant speeches to the cabinet, House of Commons and the entire nation, Churchill emphasised his determination never to surrender. Even after 300,000 men were evacuated from Dunkirk the situation was serious, as equipment had been lost and Britain had suffered a severe defeat. However, Churchill encouraged Britain to consider Dunkirk a deliverance. His portrayal of the war in highly dramatic terms to the public helped maintain their support. For example, his 'We shall never surrender' speech and his 'Never in the history of human conflict was so much owed by so many to so few' speech after the Battle of Britain. To Churchill it was vital that the momentum of war should be maintained. Therefore he made it clear to the cabinet that Britain should not even investigate possible peace terms. He even offered political union to France, as well as stating his willingness to commit more troops in order to keep France fighting until he was dissuaded from this by the commanders of the RAF and army.

By the end of 1940 Britain had survived the fall of France, the Battle of Britain and was winning some victories against the Italians in North Africa, so Churchill's stance was being justified by events.

Churchill's style of leadership

Churchill believed his role was not just to chair discussions, but to direct the war effort. In his memoirs he wrote that from 10 May 1940 'I had the ability to give directions over the whole scene'. He favoured daring ideas and actions, and was frustrated by any delays or signs of weakness. However, he could take advice and did not insist on his every idea being put into practice. Indeed, he took advice from those he thought exceptional and talented like Lord Beaverbrook and the scientist Frederick Lindemann, as well as from professional civil servants and military leaders. He believed in the power of personal contacts and relationships, and pursued an energetic series of meetings with his allies and his generals. He also respected the political system and reported regularly to the House of Commons, accepting debates on his conduct of the war and motions of censure throughout the war. He demanded complete dedication from all in public office, and he worked well into the night, often tiring out his secretaries and military leaders.

He was personally flamboyant, appearing in military uniforms to which he was not entitled and a variety of hats and costumes in order to capture the public's need for a vivid and dynamic leader. He could also be ruthless: he undermined and dismissed military leaders in whom he had lost confidence. He also supported some extreme measures in the war, like the destruction of the French fleet at Oran in 1940 and the civilian bombing of Germany. However, he often showed a warmth and loyalty to those who worked for him, and he maintained his sense of humour. He was also personally brave, wanting to go over to France with the invasion force in June 1944, and having little care for his personal safety during the bombing raids on London.

Spot the inference

High-level answers avoid just summarising or paraphrasing the sources, and instead make inferences from the sources. Below are a source, a question and a series of statements. Read Source A and decide which of the statements

- make an inference from the source (I)
- paraphrase the source (P)
- summarise the source (S)
- cannot be justified from the source (X).

How useful is Source A as evidence for Churchill's stance on the war in 1940?

Statement	I	P	S	X
The main reason for not negotiating was that we would lose the fleet.				
Churchill took a strong stance. He claimed that it was silly to think that Britain would get terms as it would lose its fleet and become controlled as a puppet state by Hitler.				
Churchill said that it was better not to surrender and that we should go on and fight it out and if Britain's story came to an end then it would be better if everyone was rolling on the ground choking on their own blood.				
Churchill's stance was based on rational calculation as he thought that Hitler would demand the fleet and that his domination of Europe would mean a loss of real independence. However, his stance was also based on a sense of national pride and a feeling for the great 'story' of Britain. He also showed great emotion by rallying the cabinet members through a highly charged image of him fighting to the last and 'choking on his own blood'.				

SOURCE A

Churchill addresses junior cabinet ministers on 28 May 1940 about negotiating a peace. The speech was noted by Hugh Dalton, a Labour minister who was present. From Hugh Dalton, The Fateful Years: Memoirs, 1931–1945.

It is idle to think that if we tried to make peace now we should get any better terms from Germany than if we went on and fought it out. The Germans would demand our fleet. We would become a slave state through a British government which would be Hitler's puppet. On the other hand, we have immense resources and advantages. Therefore we shall go on and fight it out and if at last this long story is to end, it were better it should end not through surrender but only when we are rolling senseless on the ground when each of us lies choking on our own blood.

 Using provenance and own knowledge

When answering the question above, consider the following:

- What would you say was important about the circumstances in which the speech was made?
- Who is it being spoken to and why?

 Recommended reading

- Gordon Corrigan, *Blood Sweat Tears and Arrogance*, pages 177–200
- Samantha Heywood, *Churchill*, chapters 4 and 5
- Roy Jenkins, *Churchill*
- Mike Wells and Nick Fellows, *Britain 1930–1997*, 2015 edition, pages 32–34
- Cabinet minutes, May 1940, http://www.nationalarchives.gov.uk

Churchill and his generals

What determined Churchill's attitudes to his generals and military chiefs?

Churchill was conscious that the political leaders had lost control over military strategy during the First World War and had taken too much notice of military leaders like Haig, so he wanted to avoid this. He was also very aware that the military chiefs had been cautious and had justified the failed policies of Appeasement in the 1930s.

Churchill was unusual as a prime minister in having military experience and this made him confident in trying to influence military policy, even though this experience was very out of date. He admired 'men of action' like Bernard Law Montgomery and natural leaders like Harold Alexander. He was impatient of generals who were, in his view, over-cautious, and was on bad terms with some very able men like General **Auchinleck**, whose preparations made the victory at El Alamein possible but who was dismissed nonetheless.

How well did Churchill work with his military chiefs?

Churchill's main dealings were with the senior military figure, Sir Alan Brooke. Brooke was a dogged opponent of some ill-planned and 'wildcat' schemes favoured by the Prime Minister and the men had a stormy relationship. However, despite disputes about many aspects of the war, Brooke, his fellow leaders and Churchill did agree on a basic strategy – that of focusing the land war on the Mediterranean and delaying the opening of a second front in Europe until the chances of victory seemed strong. Brooke played a vital part in the war planning and in training and deploying British forces. He had hoped to lead the invasion of France in 1944 but the less experienced US General Eisenhower was put in charge and Churchill did little to recognise and sympathise with Brooke's disappointment.

There are examples of Churchill's misjudgement and ingratitude. The success of the Battle of Britain in 1940 owed much to the strategy of Sir Hugh Dowding. By keeping the RAF in small units and avoiding pursuit of German planes after raids, he kept the RAF strong enough to meet the German attacks. His rivals had suggested a more dramatic 'big wing' policy of massing the RAF's strengths. Dowding was an uncommunicative leader who did not engage Churchill's sympathies and he was removed from his command in November 1940.

Perhaps Churchill's most important misjudgement concerned Sir Claude Auchinleck. Churchill was anxious for a rapid attack on German forces in North Africa in 1942 but Auchinleck demanded strong preparations and also a defensive fallback if the attack failed. Given the importance of maintaining control of Egypt, the **Suez Canal** and the oil fields of the Middle East, this was sensible. However, Churchill insisted on Auchinleck's removal, and after his favoured candidate, 'Strafer' Gott, was killed in a plane crash, approved the appointment of the more flamboyant and egocentric Montgomery. Montgomery's victory at El Alamein owed much to Auchinleck. This defeat of one of Hitler's most successful generals, Rommel, who had previously dominated the war in North Africa, was a major turning point in the war.

In the end, Churchill did not control over-confident and dubious military plans endorsed by Montgomery any more than Lloyd George had managed to control Haig in the First World War. For example, in 1944, to speed the final collapse of Germany, an ill-judged campaign to take the Rhine bridges at Arnhem, Nijmegen and Eindhoven was launched.

Overall, there were examples of support, encouragement, frank and lively debate and mutual respect which appear in the memoirs of military leaders who worked closely with Churchill, as well as examples of bad temper, lack of consideration, over-expectation and bullying.

Churchill lent his support to the extensive D-Day preparations, including the development of the prefabricated Mulberry harbours, and the campaign of deception to persuade the Germans that the landings would be in the Pas de Calais region and not Normandy. He always encouraged innovative military thinking and daring ideas.

Doing reliability well

Below are an exam-style question and a set of definitions listing common reasons why sources can be unreliable. Using Sources A–D below, for each source write a critical account of whether it is a reliable or unreliable piece of evidence, justifying your answer by referring to the definitions below.

Using these four sources in their historical context assess how far they support the view that Churchill did not work effectively with his generals in the period 1940 to 1945.

- Vested interest: the source is written so that the writer can protect his own power or interests.
- Second-hand report: the writer is not in a position to know and is relying on someone else's information.
- Expertise: the source is written on a subject on which the author is an expert.
- Political bias: the source is written by a politician and it reflected their political views.
- Reputation: the source is written to protect the writer's reputation.

SOURCE A

Field Marshall Wavell expresses his view of Churchill's military outlook in a letter from 1950. Quoted in Gordon Corrigan, Blood, Sweat and Arrogance: The Myths of Churchill's War.

The prime minister thought that because a comparatively small number of mounted Boers had held up a British division in 1899 or 1900 during the Boer War in South Africa, it was unnecessary for the South African brigade under my command to have any more equipment than rifles before taking the field in 1940. Winston's tactical ideas had to some extent crystallized at the South African War of 1899.

SOURCE B

General Sir Hastings Ismay, Churchill's Chief of Staff, writes to General Auchinleck in 1941. From The Memoirs of Lord Ismay.

Churchill is frank in speech and writing, but expects others to be equally frank with him. Do not be irritated with telegrams on every kind of topic, many of which may be irrelevant and superfluous.

SOURCE C

Sir Alan Brooke, Britain's most senior commander, writes about his relations with Churchill in his diary on 24 May 1943. From Alanbrooke War Diaries 1939-1945: Field Marshall Lord Alanbrooke.

Churchill thinks one thing at one moment and another at another moment. At times he thinks the war can be won by bombing. At other times it is essential for us to bleed ourselves dry on the continent because Russia is doing it. At others our main effort must be in the Balkans. More often than not he wants to carry out ALL operations simultaneously irrespective of shortages of shipping.

SOURCE D

In a telegram written on 15 January 1942, Churchill encourages General Wavell in his defence of Singapore. Quoted from Nigel Knight, Churchill. The Greatest Briton Unmasked.

Is everything being prepared? It has always seemed to me that the vital need is to prolong the defence of Singapore to the last possible minute. Everyone here is very pleased with the telegrams you have sent which give us all the feeling how buoyantly you are grappling with your tremendous task.

Churchill and the Mediterranean Strategy

The importance of the Mediterranean

Preventing Axis victories in the Mediterranean was important to Britain. The Suez Canal was an important link to India and the parts of the Empire in south-east Asia and Australasia and Britain obtained most of its oil supplies from the Middle East.

In 1940 Britain had won some quick victories against Italy, but when Hitler sent a German army to north Africa, there was a threat to Egypt and the Middle East which had to be met. Once that had been defeated in 1942–43, the chance arose for an attack on Germany through Italy and also opening a Balkan front. This was seen as an alternative to a costly attack in northern France.

Thus a lot of the British war effort took place in north Africa and later in an invasion of Sicily and then Italy. The USA was persuaded to support this. The invasion of northern France did not take place until June 1944.

Why did the Mediterranean take priority?

Churchill thought that a delay in invading France would benefit the Allies, as Germany would then be weakened by US and British bombing raids as well as from losses of troops in the USSR. He also did not think that the invasion of France would be delayed by long, as Mussolini's regime in Italy was weak and the invasion of Sicily had gone well in 1943, indicating that the campaign in Italy would be over quickly. Churchill also wanted to extend British influence in south-east Europe – something he considered strategically important for Britain.

Why were there objections?

Both American military chiefs, especially General Marshall, and Stalin objected as:

- Germany could only be defeated by invading the homeland and engaging with the bulk of the German forces. This meant invading northern France.
- Up to 1942, German defences along the French coastline of the Channel were not very developed. The great Atlantic Wall of fortifications along the coast was not built until later, so Britain was losing an opportunity.

- The idea of invading Germany through Italy or southern Europe was deemed flawed. Military theory stresses engagement at crucial points, not peripheral theatres.
- Fighting in the Mediterranean took away valuable resources, especially landing craft, from other campaigns for what was, at best, peripheral to the main struggle.

Who was right?

Churchill was correct in that the defence of oil supplies was absolutely crucial and the British had to prevent the Germans linking their forces in north Africa with their armies in southern Russia in 1941–42. The defeat of Rommel, the German commander in north Africa, required a large build up of forces. After the Germans had withdrawn from north Africa, however, the situation was less clear.

The invasion of Italy did indeed tie up valuable US and British forces. It was also not over as quickly as anticipated and instead became a long, hard struggle as the war in Italy got bogged down in **trench warfare**. German forces first reinforced Italian forces and then took over the fighting when Italy withdrew from the war. Britain also got distracted by having to take part in a civil war in Greece in 1944.

As for the impact of the delayed invasion of France, by 1944 the Germans had built formidable defences on the French coast and relations with Stalin had been weakened by the failure to open a second front in Europe. He blamed heavy Russian casualties on Britain and the USA's delay in invading France. However, an invasion needed a very large build-up of forces, as was illustrated by a raid on the French Channel port of Dieppe in 1942, which showed the problems of landing forces without great superiority of resources. By 1944, Germany had been weakened by the war in the east and there were German forces tied down in Italy. Since the war in France and Germany from 1944–45 produced casualties comparable to those of the First World War, an earlier invasion might have been very costly.

The Mediterranean Strategy remains controversial today.

Add your own knowledge

Below is an exam-style question and Sources A–D. In one colour, draw links between the sources to show ways in which they agree about the Mediterranean Strategy. In another colour draw links where they disagree. Around the edge of the sources, write relevant own knowledge. Again draw links to show the ways in which this agrees or disagrees with the sources.

Using these four sources in their historical context assess how far they support the view that Churchill's Mediterranean Strategy was flawed.

SOURCE A

Britain's senior general advises Churchill on the importance of the Mediterranean. Adapted from a memorandum by Sir John Dill on 6 May 1941.

The loss of Egypt would be a calamity but it would not end the war. The defence of the United Kingdom must take first place. Egypt is not even second in the order of priority, for it has been an accepted principle in our strategy that in the last resort the security of Singapore comes before that of Egypt.

SOURCE B

The leading US general gives his view of how the war should be fought. George Marshall, memorandum 1 April 1942.

A British-American attack through Western Europe provides the only feasible method for employing the power of the USA, the United Kingdom and Russia in a concerted attack against a single enemy.

SOURCE C

Churchill recalls explaining his view of the priorities of wartime strategy to the US in April 1942. Churchill, The Hinge of Fate, 1951.

I had to place this point of view before the American envoys. It was not possible for us to lay aside our other duties. Our first imperial obligation was to defend India against the Japanese. To allow Germany and Japan to join hands in India or the Middle East involved a measureless disaster.

SOURCE D

A report of a meeting between the US Secretary of State and President Roosevelt. Conversation, August 1942 (from Britain 1930–1997, Hodder p44).

Secretary of State Stimson warned the President that the indirect British approach, which he labeled 'pinprick warfare', would not work. If left in British hands, the cross channel invasion would never take place, for the shadows of World War One still hung too heavily over the imagination of Churchill.

Further Reading on Churchill's wartime strategy

- Mike Wells and Nicholas Fellows, *Britain 1930–1997*, p42–44 (2015)
- David Reynolds, *In Command of History*, p373–388, (2004)
- Roy Jenkins, *Churchill*, p711–714, (2001)
- Cleve Ponting *Armageddon*, p108–134, (1995)

Churchill and the bombing campaign

Why did Britain devote so many of its resources in bombing Germany?

- The German destruction of British cities in the **Blitz** caused resentment, so when Britain was able to retaliate with even more airpower and with US support this seemed justified revenge.
- For much of the war, Britain was not fighting the bulk of the German forces on land. The war was fought at sea and in the air, so bombing became the only real way of striking at Germany itself.
- There was a strong belief in **Bomber Command** that bombing was the way to win the war and to prevent large scale casualties. Though the losses of aircrew were very high in the bombing raids, it was thought worthwhile because the alternative would be British land forces facing a well-armed and equipped German army. If the bombing could reduce German military capacity then it would be saving British forces from the sort of tremendous casualties that were endured in the fighting against Germany on the Western Front during the First World War.
- There was also the implicit belief that the terror bombing of German cities would hit morale and somehow show the weakness of the Nazi regime which had consistently boasted that it would defend its citizens. The RAF developed sophisticated techniques of maximizing the effect of incendiary bombing of cities.

What was the impact?

- Far more Germans died in bombing raids than British civilians. British losses were around 60,500, but between 400,000 and 600,000 Germans were killed.
- The losses of RAF Bomber Command were heavy.
- The results were not decisive in terms of destroying either German morale or productive capacity.
- The greatest effect was when bombing was heavily concentrated on transport and communication.

- The bombing led to accusations of unnecessary and vindictive attacks on civilians. The bombing of Dresden was particularly controversial as the city was crowded with refugees and not an important military target.

What was Churchill's attitude to the bombing of civilians?

Churchill supported initiatives to bomb key German military and industrial targets, such as the famous Dambusters raid which had targeted the dams in the industrial Ruhr area of Germany, and he also supported the bombing of more civilian targets. He had been distressed at the effects of the Blitz on Britain and had visited affected areas, so revenge may have played a part in his motives for approving bombing German civilian targets.

Churchill was aware of the devastation brought about by German bombing of civilians in Poland, the Netherlands and France as a successful tactic to disrupt resistance in the early part of the war and hoped that bombing German cities would have a similar impact. He may have been over-influenced by optimistic estimates of the effects of bombing – a common view at the time – and he enthusiastically supported bombing raids, such as the heavy raid on Cologne in May 1943. In public, Churchill was dismissive of criticism of bombing on ethical grounds such as that made by Bishop Bell of Chichester. However, in private he expressed concerns about Dresden and the policy of terror bombing later in the war. Bomber Command and its leader, Arthur Harris, did not receive the public acknowledgement that the other branches of the RAF did.

Explain the differences by using provenance

The following sources give different views about the bombing of Germany. Identify what the views are and explain the differences by using the provenance of the sources. Think about the circumstances, the nature of the evidence and the context.

Questions for Source A:

What does the source show about Churchill's view of bombing?

Why and to whom was the speech made?

What was happening in the war when the speech was made?

Questions for Source B:

What does the source show about Churchill's view of bombing?

Why was the memo produced and to whom was it addressed?

What was happening in the war when it was written?

SOURCE A

Churchill speaks on 30 June 1943 at the Guildhall in London after receiving the freedom of the City of London in praise of the British bombing campaign.

Those who sowed the wind are reaping the whirlwind. In the first half of the year which ends today, the RAF alone has cast upon Germany thirty-five times the tonnage of bombs which has been discharged on this island in the same six months. Not only has the weight of our offensive bombing grown and its accuracy multiplied, but our measures of defence, tactical and scientific have improved beyond compare. In one single hour we discharged upon Dusseldorf, to take an example, 200 tons of explosive and incendiary bombs.

SOURCE B

In March 1945, Churchill writes confidentially to his senior RAF commanders after the bombing of Dresden.

It seems to me that the moment has come when the question of bombing German cities simply for the sake of increasing the terror, though under other pretexts, should be reviewed. Otherwise we shall come under control of a ruined land – the destruction of Dresden remains a serious query against the conduct of allied bombing.

Using your own knowledge

In order to find evidence for a possible source-based question on Churchill as a military leader, write two extended paragraphs using your own knowledge and material from this chapter.

- Paragraph one will show Churchill's strengths and should include four examples of his contribution to victory.
- Paragraph two will show Churchill's weaknesses and should include four examples of his lack of judgement.

Churchill, the plans for reconstruction and the 1945 election

Reasons for post-war planning

Despite being at war, Churchill's Government devoted time, thought and money to what would happen afterwards. It was fairly clear that Britain would not lose the war by 1944, so there could be thought about the post-war period without taking resources away from the war effort. The Government was also conscious that there had been disappointment when plans for a better Britain were not implemented after the First World War, so it wanted to do better this time. It was important for morale to give the British people a sense of hope that, after the defeat of Germany, there would not simply be a return to the hardships of the 1930s, and that wartime shortage, losses and sacrifice would not be in vain.

The nature of the Government itself was important. The wartime ministry was a coalition and contained Labour, Liberal and some progressive Conservative MPs and ministers who were keen to consider domestic policies alongside international ones. Churchill himself had been an active social reformer before the First World War and, though he was more concerned with military and diplomatic matters, he did not block discussion of reform at home.

Key wartime policies

There were several key domestic policies during the war that were to influence what would happen afterwards.

- There was agreement that the Beveridge Report of 1942, which proposed a 'cradle to grave' plan for social welfare to eliminate poor health, ignorance and poverty, should be enacted.
- There was a commitment to ending the old system of help for the poor and to create a new system of National Assistance.
- There were influential reports on town planning and industrial development.
- Hospitals and railways were run by the state.
- National Insurance had been reformed and a new ministry created to run it.
- The Education Act of 1944 reorganised education, ended fees and promised to raise the school leaving age to 15.

Churchill was not enthusiastic about creating a new **welfare state** but had accepted key measures and recommendations. In the event, these were instituted by Labour, who won the election of 1945.

Reasons for Labour's election victory in 1945

Labour won the 1945 election due to a combination of its own appeal and popular dislike of the Conservatives. Labour fought a well-focused campaign stressing domestic change which appealed to a general public who did not want a return to the hardships of the 1930s. Labour ministers had been more important than Conservatives in domestic affairs during the war, and were thought more likely to pass reforms after the war. Many of the state-intervention policies which were seen to work well during the war were more attributed to Labour, and the general public had become more used to the increased role of the state. In addition, members of the armed forces had become more aware of political issues and now favoured Labour.

In contrast, the Conservative's election campaign was less well organised than Labour's. It was heavily reliant on Churchill's reputation, but this was built on war-time success. Many in working-class areas remembered Churchill being opposed to strikes and **socialism**, and the Conservative Party was often associated with the unemployment and hardship of the 1930s. Churchill did not help the situation when he made an unwise speech about Labour needing a 'Gestapo' to enforce its policies, which made him unpopular.

In then end, Labour won 47 per cent of the votes and 61 per cent of the seats – the biggest Labour victory ever.

Mind map

When considering the question below, it is helpful to consider the possible causes of Churchill's defeat in the 1945 election. Complete the mind map below and explain these factors by adding information from the page opposite and your own knowledge.

Using these sources in their historical context, assess how far they support the view that Churchill was most to blame for the loss of the 1945 election.

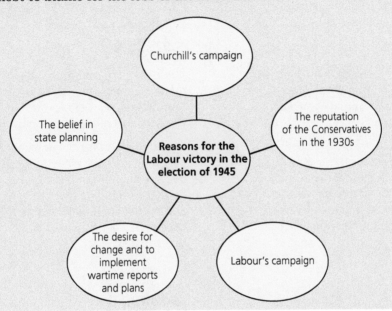

Add your own knowledge

a

Below are a question and Sources A–C. In one colour draw links between the sources to show ways in which they agree about whether Churchill was most to blame. In another colour draw links to show how they disagree. Around the edge of the source write relevant own knowledge using the mind map, your own knowledge and information from the page opposite.

Using these sources in their historical context, assess how far they support the view that Churchill was most to blame for the loss of the 1945 election.

SOURCE A

In a memorandum to Cabinet in 1943, Churchill warns his ministers about promising too much internal reform after the war, following the Beveridge Report.

Ministers should in my view be careful not to raise false hopes as was done last time (during World War One) by speeches about 'homes fit for heroes'. It is for this reason of not raising false hopes and airy visions of Utopia and Eldorado that I have refrained from making promises about the future.

SOURCE B

Raymond Mortimer, a Labour MP, writes on 10 July 1945 to the Conservative MP Harold Nicolson about Churchill and the election of 1945.

I think that more than anyone else Churchill was responsible for the squalid lies in these elections. He started the rot with his talk of Mr Attlee's Gestapo. I should like to see Mr Churchill retire. I think him quite wrong for the reconstruction of England.

SOURCE C

Churchill's private secretary gives his view of the likely result of the election. From Sir John Colville, The Fringes of Power: Downing Street Diaries, 1939–1955.

The Prime Minister's speech was a fighting and provocative effort. Labour propaganda is better and it links to the popular mood. I think the Service vote (i.e. the vote by the armed services) will be for Labour and the housing shortage has left many people disgruntled.

Exam focus

Below is a series of sources and an exam-style question. Read the sources, question and model response as well as the comments around the essay.

Using these four sources in their historical context assess the view that Churchill was a great wartime leader.★

★(At AS-level, Source C would be omitted)

SOURCE A

Churchill's Chief of Staff recalls working with him during the Second World War. From Lord Ismay, The Memoirs of General Lord Ismay, *1960.*

Churchill was certainly frank in his speech and writing, and expected others to be equally frank with him. No commander who engaged the enemy ever need fear that he would not be supported. His knowledge of military history was immense and his broad sweep of strategy was unrivalled.

SOURCE B

A left-wing critic of Churchill who later became an influential minister in the Labour Government of 1945 offers a view of his wartime leadership. Aneurin Bevan, Churchill by his Contemporaries, *1965.*

Churchill's greatest contributions were to persuade people not to look at facts. When the people of the country might have been depressed about Dunkirk, he was persuading them to think of Queen Elizabeth and the defeat of the Armada in 1588. He put the case of Britain to the world and the destiny of Britain to the British.

SOURCE C

The military assistant secretary to the Cabinet reflects on Churchill as a war leader. General Sir Ian Jacob, Action this Day, *1968.*

Churchill tended to think of 'sabre and bayonet'. He did not understand that infantry had little power unless properly organised with good communications. He did not fully understand the changes that had taken place since the First World War. However, he had an interest in new inventions. He kept fully abreast of developments in radar, in aerial navigation. Nothing fell outside his enquiring mind.

SOURCE D

British senior soldier Sir Alan Brooke writes about a wartime military conference in his diary, 19 August 1943. From Alanbrooke War Diaries 1939-1945: Field Marshall Lord Alanbrooke.

Another poisonous day! The Prime Minister behaved like a spoilt child that wants a toy in a shop, regardless of the fact that its parents tell him that it is no good. Got nowhere with him and settled nothing. He shook his fist in my face and said 'I do not want any of your long term plans, they stifle initiative!' This made arguing impossible.

Churchill has a reputation as an inspirational wartime leader and this is expressed in Source B. The other sources are more critical, but Source C does show some of his strengths as an open-minded and innovative leader, though it is critical of his old-fashioned outlook. While Source A hints that Churchill could be difficult, his knowledge and military understanding, necessary attributes of a great war leader, are praised. Source D, however, reveals a leader who is not really great, but rather unrealistic and irritable.

Of the sources which praise Churchill, Source B is the most unexpected. Bevan was a left-winger and might have been expected to object to Churchill as a Conservative and someone opposed to socialism. He is writing sometime after the war and would have been conscious of Churchill's contribution to the overthrow of Nazism. He also was not in government so would not have had the personal knowledge of Churchill of the other sources. As a politician he praises Churchill's gifts of communication both to the British public and to the world. In saying that he persuaded people not to look at facts, then he is accurate. In 1940 Britain stood alone in Europe against Germany. The situation was desperate enough for some cabinet members to consider asking what terms Hitler might offer. The British had suffered a disaster in France and Germany and the USSR were allied. There was little hope of the USA entering the war, but Churchill still spoke of victory being the British aim. This heroic stance and the ability to rally international and national opinion were rightly seen as greatness, though Bevan is not in a position to see how Churchill operated on a day-to-day basis. This is very much Churchill the public figure.

Ismay in Source A did work closely with the Prime Minister and this did not stop him praising Churchill's support for his commanders and his military abilities. However, it was not written during the war but in 1960. Churchill did support some of his generals, notably Montgomery and Alexander, but not all. Some generals like Auchinleck and Wavell, despite winning victories or preparing for victory, were not supported. Also, Churchill was not always a master of strategy. The long struggle through Italy from 1943 to 1945 was not well thought-out, for instance. Probably the fairest judgement here is Churchill's knowledge of military history as he had made a study of his ancestor Marlborough.

Source C is more balanced. Churchill's military experience did go back to the late nineteenth century and he was always impressed by daring – sometimes leading to poor decisions like the Dieppe Raid of 1942 and neglecting military back up. Jacob in Source C balances this by Churchill's interest in innovations and he did promote some key ideas like the Mulberry Harbours at D-Day and the deceptions that led the Germans to think the invasion would be in the Pas de Calais. Jacob knew Churchill well but again is writing after the war in a book to celebrate his life.

Source D on the other hand is written in the heat of the moment and after a tiring and irritating meeting. He speaks of Churchill's immaturity and his aggressive behaviour, something not mentioned in the other sources. Brooke and Churchill had many such quarrels. In 1943 Britain had begun the long fight back, but the war was a long way from being won and the strain on both the Prime Minister and his generals was considerable. This may be an immediate response rather than a considered judgement but it does show that Churchill could be difficult to work worth, something hinted at in Source A when Ismay talks about his frankness.

There is no requirement to group sources, but this overview is helpful.

The analysis of Source B considers both the provenance and includes some contextual knowledge and does offer some judgement about the validity of the view.

In looking at Source A, the answer looks at provenance, for example when it was written, and also applies knowledge to assess its validity.

There is some knowledge applied to Source C and its provenance is considered.

The answer looks at the nature of Source D and tries to put it into context. Brooke spoke more warmly about Churchill elsewhere but this is not necessary to know.

A link is made to Source A.

Churchill did communicate wonderfully in public as Source B says, and his greatness lies more in that than in the detailed running of the war, where he was too inclined to interfere, as Source D says, and did not have an up-to-date understanding of the needs of modern warfare, as is shown, for example, in his impatience for an attack on Rommel in Egypt in the autumn of 1942. The truth may therefore be that Churchill was not always a great war leader but his leadership certainly had elements of greatness.

Though this might have been more developed there is a judgement made based on the sources.

This is a very strong answer. All four sources are considered, and there is analysis of their provenance. Well-selected contextual knowledge is also used intelligently. The answer is well organised and has some final judgement, and the focus on the question is maintained.

Understanding the demands of the question

In different colours, underline examples where the answer uses own knowledge, evaluates, quotes from the sources and cross-references the sources.

AS question

The following is an AS-type question on one source and model answer.

Use your knowledge of the situation in 1940 to assess how useful Source B (see page 30) is about Churchill's greatness as a war leader.

Source B argues that it was Churchill's lack of realism that made him a great leader and that he managed to persuade the British people not to look at facts but to have the confidence to believe in the destiny of Britain to be the defenders of good over evil and the survival of the British race. The source suggests that Britain might have been depressed about Dunkirk but he prevented this by stressing the greatness of the British past (Queen Elizabeth and the defeat of the Armada) and that he was able to influence international opinion by making it appear that Britain was fighting for a great cause and defending the values of civilisation.

This source, taken not from a supporter but an opponent, is useful in explaining the role Churchill played in the context of a dangerous situation and does not exaggerate his role. The situation in 1940 certainly supports the view that it was necessary for the British people to maintain confidence and morale. The German armies had invaded the Low Countries, had occupied Denmark and defeated British forces in Norway. When they invaded France, British forces were cut off from the much larger French army and were threatened with utter destruction. Though 300,000 troops were evacuated from Dunkirk, their equipment was left behind and Churchill was unable to persuade France to fight on. So there was every reason to feel depressed by Dunkirk. But it was made into a heroic episode so seen not as humiliating defeat but a victory.

Churchill was able by his speeches in 1940 to stress the heroic nature of carrying on war when logic suggested that Britain make peace, as her army had been driven out of France, her major ally had collapsed, Russia was allied to Hitler and Mussolini, Japan was a threat in Asia and the USA showed no signs of intervening. It was important to put the case for carrying on to the British people as the source says because as Churchill told the cabinet, German terms would mean a loss of independence and the navy and an end to 'our island story'. Churchill thought that if the war continued, sooner or later the USA, joined to Britain by race and culture, would come to its aid. Thus influencing US and Empire opinion by heroic, defiant speeches insisting that Britain had only one aim of victory and would fight by all means was very important and marks Churchill out as a great war leader. Even though Bevan was a political opponent he realised this, even if the tribute is a little 'back handed' by saying in effect that Churchill did not face the facts. There is a view that the facts made it imperative to carry on the struggle, born out by the ability of Britain to achieve victories against the German airforce later in 1940 and in North Africa against Italy.

This is a clear explanation of what the source is saying and links to the question.

There is contextual knowledge of the situation in 1940 applied to the source.

This deals well with the source's stress on putting the case to the world and its importance.

The answer is aware of the nuanced judgement in the source.

More practice

Use your knowledge of the situation in 1940 to assess how useful Source C (see page 30) is about Churchill's greatness as a war leader.

3 Churchill and international diplomacy, 1939–51

How Churchill viewed Britain's world and imperial role

How did Churchill view Britain's international role in the Second World War?

Winston Churchill saw Britain as a major world power that had entered the Second World War to maintain peace and to honour its obligations. The balance of power had been threatened by German expansion, and after the guarantee to Poland in March 1939 Britain had, as a leading power, a moral obligation to go to war, whatever the cost. For Churchill, Britain was a great power because of its extensive empire. He believed in the British Empire as a force for good and he thought that the Empire would fight alongside Britain. In addition, Churchill believed that the 'English-speaking peoples', the Anglo-Saxon world community including the USA and the dominions in the Empire, had natural bonds and would stand together to defend democracy and freedom. Before the war, Churchill had urged an alliance between the opponents of the expansionist powers, Germany, Italy and Japan. The alliance during the war confirmed his belief in 'the United Nations', as the alliance was called, acting together to prevent aggression. The term 'United Nations' was later applied to the organisation formed after the war to replace the League of Nations as a world body for maintaining peace.

Churchill's view of empire

Churchill believed in the common interests of Britain and the white dominions, and he relied on their wartime support. He consulted with statesmen from the dominions and appointed high-ranking military leaders from the dominions. These played a major role in Britain's military success.

Churchill's view of the colonies was very different. Though he had agreed to the **Atlantic Charter**, there were no plans to actually extend its democratic principles to those parts of the Empire which were not majority white. The British colonies were expected to provide troops and also food and raw materials for the war effort without getting any concessions towards greater self-government. British rule in India was enforced through the war and the leaders of the Quit India campaign were imprisoned. There were no wartime promises of independence and the role of the British government in instigating/exacerbating the Bengal famine of 1943 remains a contested topic among historians.

Churchill resented US concerns about maintaining the British Empire and restated his commitment to preserving it.

Churchill and Britain's role after 1945

The pivotal role that Britain played in standing alone against Hitler in 1940 gave Britain huge prestige. Churchill used this to ensure that Britain played a part in world affairs which was greater than her resources or her contribution to the war effort really justified. Conscious of being forced to subordinate some key decisions to the USA and having to make concessions to the USSR from 1943, Churchill did his best to maintain British influence in the final years of the war. He played a major role in a series of wartime conferences, culminating in the meetings at Yalta and Potsdam which shaped the post-war world.

Churchill saw the defeat of Japan as bringing about a return to Britain's major imperial role in south-east Asia. There was no suggestion in his mind that Britain would change its role in Asia or grant independence either to India or to the rich colonies of Malaya and Singapore.

After the war, Churchill continued to view Britain as being at the centre of international affairs and a key promoter of Western moral and democratic values. Britain was a leader in establishing the United Nations, and the first meetings of the **Security Council** and the General Assembly were held in London. His speech in the USA referring to 'the Iron Curtain' saw the continuing need of Churchill to dramatise conflict and ensure that Britain was occupying the moral high ground. He did promote European unity, wishing Britain to take the lead in ending hatred in Europe and encouraging co-operation. However, he saw Britain as having a unique position because of its history of involvement in European affairs; its special relationship with the USA and its worldwide Empire.

✦ Spot the inference

High-level answers avoid just summarising or paraphrasing the sources and instead make inferences from the sources. Below are a source, a question and a series of statements. Read Source A and decide which of the statements

- make an inference from the source (I)
- paraphrase the source (P)
- summarise the source (S)
- cannot be justified from the source (X).

How useful is Source A as evidence for Churchill's view of Britain's position in the world?

Statement	I	P	S	X
1 Conscious that Britain's allies are distrustful of its empire, Churchill stresses that the British Empire is a force for good because there is no desire to expand or take resources such as bases and oilfields. He establishes that Britain does not wish to be in conflict with other countries and her Empire is not merely a means of taking land. He feels it necessary to defend Britain's imperial position and establish its position in any future discussions about the post-war world that Britain seeks only peace.				
2 Churchill's view is that Britain does not want to seek new lands and is not envious of oilfields. He says that Britain is not asking for bases for its air force or navy. He says that Britain is not setting itself up to rival others. Britain is a well-established country and wants to live in peace.				
3 Churchill's view is that Britain is a peaceful country; that it does not want any expansion, for example to gain military bases and oilfields. That as a historic country it just wants to live in peace and is not going to be a rival to other countries and that its Empire, despite what others say, is not selfish or greedy.				
4 As Churchill wanted more territory and to gain vital oilfields he had to pretend that Britain was very peaceful and did not want extra lands.				

SOURCE A

Churchill speaks in the House of Commons in January 1945 about Britain's position as the war draws closer to an end.

We seek no territory; we covet no oilfields; we demand no bases for the forces of the air or the seas. We are an ancient Commonwealth, dwelling and wishing to dwell in peace within our own habitations. We do not set ourselves up in rivalry of bigness and might with any other community in the world. Our motives are disinterested, lofty and true. I repulse those calumnies (lies) that the British Empire is a selfish, greedy, land-hungry, designing nation.

SOURCE B

Part of the Atlantic Charter agreed by Roosevelt and Churchill as being the principles of Britain and the USA in August 1941.

Third, they respect the right of all peoples to choose the form of government under which they will live; and they wish to see sovereign rights and self-government restored to those who have been forcibly deprived of them ...

Eighth, they believe that all the nations of the world should come to the abandonment of the use of force.

✦ Assessing reliability

Look at the source question below. To help you answer it think about the following questions:

- When was it signed?
- Was it a private or a public document?
- Who would read the document?
- Why would Churchill be eager to sign a joint document with the USA at this time?

How reliable is Source B as an expression of Churchill's view of Britain's world role?

Churchill and international conferences, 1940–45

Churchill devoted considerable time to conferences between 1941 and 1945. These resulted in some very important policies being determined and also some key decisions about post-war Europe.

- The commitment to democracy as a war aim and the policy of unconditional surrender emerged from conferences with the USA.
- The Mediterranean Strategy was accepted by the USA as the major way forward in war planning.
- The decision to set D-Day in 1944 was another key decision.
- Churchill agreed with Stalin in 1944 in a Moscow meeting about spheres of influence in eastern Europe.
- The division of Germany after the war was finalised at conferences at Yalta and Potsdam.
- The decision to establish a United Nations emerged from the Yalta Conference.
- Stalin's declaration of war on Japan was decided at Yalta.

Therefore, Churchill was a major influence on the key decisions on wartime strategy, aims and also on the shape of post-war Europe.

How important a contribution did Churchill make?

Churchill achieved his aim of getting Britain's allies to accept the Mediterranean Strategy. His relations with both Roosevelt and Stalin helped to ensure that a Grand Alliance was maintained and that there was communication between the allies. This helped Britain remain a major player on the world scene, and Britain was one of the powers which occupied Germany in 1945. Churchill also managed to influence Stalin into agreeing to spheres of influence in eastern Europe and not to occupy Greece. The strength of British and US co-operation developed in wartime conferences could be demonstrated by the fact that the USA shared its major weapon development – the atomic bomb – with Britain. As Britain's contribution to the war effort was significantly less than either that of the USA or the USSR, these could be seen as major achievements.

However, there were instances of Churchill having less influence than he would have liked. It was made clear to him at the Tehran Conference of 1943 that the USA regarded Britain as a junior partner. Churchill had not wanted to sign the Atlantic Charter, given Britain's continuing desire to rule over subject people in its Empire, but had been compelled to do so in order to get US support. He had also been compelled to accept territorial changes in Poland that went against Britain's moral obligations. The war was supposed to be in support of its Polish ally but Churchill had to accept Stalin's annexation of western Poland and his favouring of the unrepresentative Communist Poles. At Yalta, Churchill had to accept the return of Russian prisoners of war who had fought for the Germans to the USSR, even though it was clear that they would be killed or imprisoned on their return. Stalin would not join in the war against Japan until it was clear that Japan was bound to be defeated and a rapid invasion would give the USSR gains, probably at Britain's expense.

The sheer amount of travel involved in the conferences and the strain of maintaining unity would have weakened a much younger man. Churchill overestimated his influence with the USA and was forced into appeasing the USSR, but he did achieve a lot given that Britain was 'punching above its weight'.

Add your own knowledge

Below is an exam-style question and Sources A–D, all of which are taken from a House of Commons debate in February 1945. In one colour, draw links between the sources to show ways in which they agree. In another colour draw links where they disagree. Around the edge of the sources, write relevant own knowledge. Again draw links to show the ways in which this agrees or disagrees with the sources.

Using these sources in their historical context, assess the view that Churchill did not treat Poland fairly at the Yalta Conference on 1945.

SOURCE A

The Prime Minister defends the settlement made at Yalta regarding Poland. House of Commons debate, February 1945.

In supporting the Russian claim to the Curzon Line, I repudiate and repulse any suggestion that we are making a questionable compromise or yielding to force or fear, and I assert with the utmost conviction the broad justice of the policy upon which, for the first time, all the three great Allies have now taken their stand. Moreover, the three Powers have now agreed that Poland shall receive substantial accessions of territory both in the North and in the West.

SOURCE B

Sir Alec Douglas-Home, a Conservative MP who would later become Prime Minister in the 1960s, is critical. House of Commons debate, February 1945.

I feel certain misgivings about the Yalta agreement; a Europe of small, free, independent States is a fundamental British interest, and we interpret this Clause as covering the right of Poland and other sovereign States to real independence. We could never be a party to a process under which a whole range of the smaller countries of Europe was drawn, by a mixture of military pressure from without and political disruption from within, into the orbit of another and a greater Power.

SOURCE C

Denis Pritt, a left-wing Labour MP, defends the Yalta settlement. House of Commons debate, February 1945.

From a general view, the achievements of the Crimea Conference are perhaps among the most hopeful things that have happened in the world in the last 25 years or more.

It would be most unfortunate if we spent half of this debate discussing Poland. Enmity and suspicion of the Soviet Union have done more in the last 25 years to bring about wars than anything else except Fascism.

SOURCE D

Captain John McEwen, a Scottish Conservative MP, expresses his view. House of Commons debate, February 1945.

What has been done about Poland in the Crimea Conference has been done, but I for one cannot join in the chorus of approval which has greeted its doing, I feel I cannot allow it to pass without registering a definite but uncompromising protest. Russian interests have been allowed to prevail.

Essay planning

Plan a mini-essay for the following question:

How well did Churchill manage relations with the USA between 1940 and 1945?

- Find four pieces of evidence from this book and your own reading to show that he was not very successful and explain them.
- Find four pieces of evidence from this book and your own reading to show that he was successful and explain them.
- Write a conclusion based on these points.

Churchill's relations with other wartime leaders

The three key leaders during the Second World War were Roosevelt (USA), Stalin (USSR) and de Gaulle (France).

How well did Churchill deal with Roosevelt?

Relations between Britain and the USA in 1939–41 were mixed. On the one hand, Roosevelt would not commit the USA to giving direct aid for Britain but Britain was allowed to buy arms and it gained 50 US destroyers in return for naval bases. From March 1941, the **Lease-Lend** programme gave Britain war materials and credit. The USA did provide more direct help through its navy patrolling a neutral zone in the Atlantic to protect merchant shipping from German attacks. When Churchill met Roosevelt at Placentia Bay in August 1941 and agreed common principles in the Atlantic Charter, he established apparently warm relations with him. On the other hand, the USA drove a hard bargain. Britain had to use its gold reserves as a guarantee for Lease-Lend assistance and the 50 destroyers were too old to be of much help. In the end, it was always unlikely that Roosevelt would persuade Congress to enter the war. It was only Hitler's declaration of war on the USA in December 1941 that guaranteed the USA joining Britain against Germany.

There were many signs of a successful relationship when they were wartime allies, however. Churchill was successful in getting the USA to adopt a 'Europe First' policy of defeating Germany before Japan and to accept his Mediterranean Strategy. The USA contributed enormously to the invasion of northern France in 1944. Churchill and Roosevelt corresponded frequently, and met together to discuss the war and the post-war settlement.

There were problems in the relationship, though, particularly during the latter part of the war when, from late 1943, Roosevelt and Churchill were less close. Roosevelt was unhappy about delaying the invasion of France and wanted to commit more resources to Japan. He also did not agree to opening another front in the Balkans. Roosevelt did not share Churchill's distrust of Stalin. Despite the apparent close ties between the two, Roosevelt never visited Britain during the war.

Churchill and Stalin

Churchill put aside his dislike of communism to welcome Stalin as an ally in 1941 but he never entirely trusted him. He went to Moscow in August 1942 but there were disagreements about opening up a second front. From 1943, Churchill was resentful when Roosevelt and Stalin appeared to be on closer terms with each other than with him.

Churchill was worried about Russian desires for expansion and made a deal with Stalin in 1944 to divide eastern Europe – the so-called Percentages Agreement. Stalin did not try to take over Greece but in practice the USSR dominated Romania, Hungary, Bulgaria and Poland, so Churchill had to accept Russian domination of eastern Europe.

Churchill and de Gaulle

Churchill admired de Gaulle's patriotism and confidence but found him difficult to work with and there were stormy meetings between the two. De Gaulle saw himself as France's natural leader but Churchill did not accept that and he was frustrated by de Gaulle's unwillingness to work with other French leaders. This became a major problem after the end of the North African campaign. De Gaulle refused to work with the French leader favoured by the US, Giraud, and resented US cooperation with French authorities in Algeria and Tunisia who had been part of the French Vichy regime which had cooperated with Germany, The rivalry between De Gaulle and Giraud threatened allied unity and caused strains at the Casablanca conference of 1943.

Doing reliability well

Below are an exam-style question and a set of definitions listing common reasons why sources can be unreliable. Using Sources A–C below, for each source write a critical account of whether it is a reliable or unreliable piece of evidence, justifying your answer by referring to the definitions below.

Using these sources in their historical context, assess the view that Churchill maintained strong relations with Roosevelt from 1941 to 1945.

- Vested interest: the source is written so that the writer can protect his own power or interests.
- Second-hand report: the writer is not in a position to know and is relying on someone else's information.
- Expertise: the source is written on a subject on which the author is an expert.
- Political bias: the source is written by a politician and it reflected their political views.
- Reputation: the source is written to protect the writer's reputation.

SOURCE A

Churchill's personal doctor recalls events at the Tehran Conference in 1943. From Lord Moran, Winston Churchill: The Struggle for Survival.

When I saw the Prime Minister he was plainly put out. It seems that he sent a note to the President suggesting they should lunch together, but the President said 'No'. This did not prevent the President seeing Stalin alone after lunch. The President hoped that British Malaya, Burma and other colonies would soon be 'educated on the arts of self government'.

SOURCE B

Franklin Roosevelt speaks about Britain to his son in 1944. From Elliott Roosevelt, As He Saw It, *1946.*

They must never get the idea we're in the war just to help them to hang on to their archaic, medieval empire. I hope they realise that we're the senior partner and we're not going to sit back after we've won and watch their system stultify the growth of every country in Asia and half the countries in Europe.

SOURCE C

Churchill, in a speech in the House of Commons in April 1945, pays tribute to Roosevelt following his death.

We drew up together the Atlantic Charter which will, I trust, long remain a guide for both our peoples. Nor need I speak of the plans which we made with our great ally Russia at Tehran. In Franklin Roosevelt there died the greatest American friend who has ever brought help and comfort from the New World to the Old.

Churchill and post-war Europe

REVISED

As a result of the war, Britain was committed to maintaining peace in post-war Europe and British forces were left running a zone of occupation in Germany. Given the losses of two world wars, greater European co-operation was important in keeping the peace, something that was in Britain's interests in every sense. Churchill saw Britain having a major role in a more united and peaceful Europe.

- He spoke in favour of greater European unity at Zurich in 1946. He believed in the concept of 'the European family' and urged a 'United States of Europe'.
- He did not see greater links with Europe as incompatible with other international links such as with the United Nations or the British Commonwealth.
- He had a history of promoting European co-operation. He had supported Ariste Briand's idea of a European union in 1930 and had offered to unite Britain and France in 1940.
- He spoke in favour of reducing trade barriers and promoting economic co-operation in Europe.
- He agreed with the establishment of the Council of Europe in 1949, with 800 influential Europeans meeting to establish a forum for co-operation.
- He was far from being either an isolationist or someone who was more interested in empire; he was a frequent visitor to Europe, and had supported involvement in two world wars to maintain the balance of power in Europe.

How great was his commitment to European union?

Despite advocating a major role for Britain in a more united Europe, Churchill still believed in Britain's imperial role and the maintenance of Empire. This involved special economic relations with Britain's Empire and Commonwealth. He also saw the relationship with the USA as essential in meeting the threat to Europe from the newly expanded USSR in the Cold War period.

Post-war Europe was still suffering from the effects of war. Germany was divided and only gradually recovering from the effects of the destruction of war. Italy, too, was struggling economically. France and Britain had not been on good terms – Britain resented the French surrender in 1940 and France remembered the sinking of the French fleet by Britain. Many French people had supported the Vichy regime and de Gaulle and his supporters had not been on good terms with Churchill. Thus Churchill saw the limitations of relying too much on Europe. He did not advocate joining post-war European organisations such as the European Coal and Steel Community and he made it clear to the Cabinet in 1951 that it was not his policy to 'become an integral part of a European Federation' and that the priority should be maintaining the Empire and Commonwealth.

Greater European co-operation was important as a means of preventing the spread of communism, preventing more conflict between France and Germany, which had led to two major wars, and increasing economic prosperity and trade. However, institutional development was not seen to be in Britain's interests and Churchill did not promote this. While not a Eurosceptic, he was not the Europhile that later advocates of union with Europe claimed.

Explain the differences by using provenance

The following sources give different evidence of Churchill's views on Europe. Identify what the views are and explain the differences by using the provenance of the sources. Think about the circumstances, the nature of the evidence and the context.

Questions for Source A:

What does the source show about Churchill's view of Europe?

Why and to whom was the speech made?

What position was Churchill in when the speech was made?

Questions for Source B:

What does the source show about Churchill's view of Europe?

Why was the memo produced and to whom was it addressed?

What was happening in Churchill's career when it was written?

SOURCE A

Churchill speaks at the University of Zurich about Europe in 1946.

I wish to speak to you about the tragedy of Europe. There is a remedy which would transform the whole scene, and would in a few years make all Europe as free and happy as Switzerland is today. It is to recreate the European family and provide a structure under which it can dwell in peace, in safety, and in freedom. We must build a kind of United States of Europe. Why should there not be a European group which could give a sense of common citizenship?

SOURCE B

Churchill gives his views to the Cabinet in 1951.

I never thought that Britain or the British Commonwealth should either individually or collectively, become an integral part of a European Federation and have not given the slightest support to the idea. Our first objective is the unity and consolidation of the Commonwealth and what is left of the former British Empire.

Using your own knowledge

Which of these statements could be used to assess how reliable Source A is as evidence for Churchill's views on Europe? Indicate by ticking the boxes in the table below

Statement	Useful	Not useful
Churchill had supported European unity in 1930.		
Churchill did not support Britain joining the European Coal and Steel Community.		
Churchill opposed Appeasement.		
Churchill was free to express his own views when he was out of office after 1945.		
Churchill had never been a 'little Englander' and was at home in Europe.		

Churchill and the Iron Curtain

In March 1946, Churchill made a speech in the USA in Fulton, Missouri that used the term 'Iron Curtain'.

What was the significance of the speech and the concept?

Though not a new term, its use by such a famous person helped to make it almost a standard way of referring to Russia and its satellite states in Eastern Europe. It helped to foster the idea of an impossible barrier between the USSR and the West. Thus, it worsened relations between Russia and the West and encouraged the view that the West needed to maintain armaments to defend itself and that negotiations with the USSR would achieve little because of the 'curtain' between Communist dictatorship and Western democracy.

The speech also reinforced Stalin's belief in Western hostility towards the USSR, despite the fact that Churchill had been willing to meet with him in the war, to praise Russia's determination, to acknowledge its sacrifice and losses and to do a deal with him about domination of eastern Europe in 1944. Stalin's response shows that he thought that the West still did not understand the Soviet need for security, despite the massive losses that the USSR had endured in the war.

The nature of the speech

The section on the Iron Curtain 'from Stettin in the Baltic to Trieste in the Adriatic', behind which lay 'Warsaw, Berlin, Prague, Vienna, Budapest, Bucharest and Sofia', was often taken out of context:

- The speech also referred to Churchill's admiration for the valiant people of Russia.
- It said that Stalin did not desire war.
- It called for a settlement.

However, it also referred to the USSR and the 'expansion of its power and doctrine', and how it only responded to 'strength' because it had no respect for weakness.

The speech did not reflect the true situation at the time:

- Berlin was divided between four powers and was not completely under Soviet control. It was run by a joint commission.
- Yugoslavia was not totally dominated by the USSR.
- Czechoslovakia was not under total Communist control in 1946.
- There was no evidence that Stalin was planning further expansion.
- Though the Red Army was a powerful influence, the total domination of eastern Europe was not complete in 1946.
- There was, as Stalin said, no acknowledgement that the USSR might have had real defence concerns in its desire to put a barrier between itself and the West.

This is not to say, however, that it was untrue that Russian policy was intent on creating a bloc of satellite states and that it had little respect for democratic elections that might threaten this.

Reactions to the speech

In the USA, opinion at the time was not universally favourable to the speech and some newspapers were critical. US policy was not transformed by the speech. President Truman was unsympathetic to both communism and the USSR. Advisers like Kennan were influential in seeing traditional Russian expansion as a threat to stability in Europe. The USA was already concerned that the domination of eastern Europe would threaten America's economic interests by creating a closed economic zone before the speech was given.

In the USSR and for many on the political left across Europe, the speech produced a very hostile reaction.

Doing reliability well

Below are an exam-style question and a set of definitions listing common reasons why sources can be unreliable. Using Sources A–C below, for each source write a critical account of whether it is a reliable or unreliable piece of evidence, justifying your answer by referring to the definitions below.

Using these sources in their historical context, assess the view that Churchill's Iron Curtain Speech of March 1946 was unwise.

- Vested interest: the source is written so that the writer can protect his own power or interests.
- Second-hand report: the writer is not in a position to know and is relying on someone else's information.
- Expertise: the source is written on a subject on which the author is an expert.
- Political bias: the source is written by a politician and it reflected their political views.
- Reputation: the source is written to protect the writer's reputation.

SOURCE A

Stalin Responds to Churchill's speech. From Pravda, *March 1946.*

Mr Churchill now stands in the position of a firebrand of war. And Mr Churchill is not alone here. He has friends not only in England but also in the United States of America. In this respect, one is reminded remarkably of Hitler and his friends.

SOURCE B

The US Ambassador in Moscow informs the US Secretary of State about the Russian reaction to Churchill's speech in March 1946.

Moscow is relieved about the general situation as reflected in the public reaction to Churchill's speech. Had his speech found greater support in English and American public opinion and government circles, Moscow would have taken a much more serious view.

SOURCE C

The US State Department informs the British Foreign Office of the impact of the speech in a message from 10 March 1946.

Americans really listen to Mr Churchill, and there is little doubt that the speech will set the pattern of discussion on world affairs. If his view is not at this stage acceptable to press and Congressional opinion, President Truman and Admiral Leahy were described as very warm in their compliments to him.

SOURCE D

Churchill delivers his 'Iron Curtain' speech at Fulton, Missouri, in March 1946.

From Stettin in the Baltic to Trieste in the Adriatic an iron curtain has descended across the continent. Behind that line lie all the capitals of the ancient states of central and Eastern Europe.

Use your own knowledge

Read Source D above and use your own knowledge to assess how reliable it is as evidence for the situation in 1946. Find two clear pieces of information to support your view.

Exam focus

Below is an exam-style source question. Read it, the sources and the model response as well as the comments around it.

Using these four sources in their historical context, assess how far they support the view that de Gaulle was most to blame for bad relations with Britain and the USA during the Second World War.

SOURCE A

De Gaulle recalls a stormy meeting with Churchill in 1942. Charles de Gaulle, Memoirs, *1956.*

Mr Churchill attacked me in a bitter and highly emotional way. When I pointed out that the establishment of a British-controlled administration in Madagascar would interfere with the rights of France, he exclaimed furiously 'You claim to be France! You are not France!'

I interrupted him, 'If in your eyes I am not representative of France, why and with what right are you dealing with me?' Mr Churchill did not reply.

SOURCE B

Churchill's doctor recalls Churchill's view of de Gaulle at the Casablanca Conference of 1943. Lord Moran, Churchill: The Struggle for Survival, *1966.*

The Prime Minister watched de Gaulle stalk down the garden with his head in the air. 'His country has given up fighting: he himself is a refugee and if we turn him down he is finished. Look at him! He might be Stalin with two hundred divisions. France without an army is not France; de Gaulle is the spirit of that army, perhaps the last survivor of that warrior race.'

SOURCE C

De Gaulle sends a telegram on 6 June 1942 to Free French commanders in Africa and the Middle East following British landings on Madagascar, a French colony, to ensure it would not be taken by the enemy.

The British are doing everything possible to take away our territory as in the Madagascar invasion. I am not prepared to remain associated with the Anglo-Saxon powers. We must form a united front against them. We must warn the French people and the whole world by radio of the Anglo-Saxon conspiracy.

SOURCE D

Churchill writes to Foreign Secretary Anthony Eden about his reluctance to allow de Gaulle to visit France in the aftermath of the D-Day landings in June 1944.

He has shown himself entirely free from any sympathy with us or the Americans or the efforts we are making to liberate his country. He would no doubt like to have a demonstration to show he is the future President of the French Republic. There is not a scrap of generosity about this man who wishes to pose as the saviour of France, without a single French solider to back him up.

De Gaulle was a self-appointed spokesman for the Free French and his confidence and patriotism were admired by Churchill, but he was difficult to deal with and Roosevelt distrusted him, preferring other French leaders. Relations were stormy, with both Churchill and de Gaulle being angry. Source A seems to show that Churchill was more to blame, as de Gaulle says that he was bitter and de Gaulle also points out that Churchill is being unreasonable in denying that de Gaulle represents France when Churchill is speaking with him as if he did. The exchange seems to favour de Gaulle and is from de Gaulle's own memoirs written some time after the war in 1956. This may make it somewhat suspect. In fact, Churchill, though not tactful, is stating the position: de Gaulle was not elected to represent France. Given the general popularity of the Vichy regime, it is unlikely that he was representative. De Gaulle had insisted that he be given resources for a raid on Vichy territory in west Africa which had failed, so this may explain Churchill's frustration. By 1944 relations have not improved. Churchill is complaining about a lack of gratitude shown by de Gaulle for the very great invasion of northern France undertaken at D-Day in June 1944 by a joint British and American invasion force. The issue is that de Gaulle saw himself as the real ruler of France since the pro German Vichy French regime had no validity. Churchill was afraid that French opinion would be alienated if de Gaulle claimed to rule even though he was totally unelected and Vichy had been seen as legitimate. In de Gaulle's defence, the D-Day landings had been considerably delayed as the USA had wanted them in 1942 and Stalin had long called for a second front. As Eden had had to put up with de Gaulle's uncompromising attitudes Churchill was writing to someone that he knew would sympathise with his view, rather than attempting to see the situation from de Gaulle's point of view. The sympathetic approach seen in C has hardened.

In C Churchill is shown as being understanding and de Gaulle is being portrayed as somewhat arrogant by Lord Moran. De Gaulle was a fighting man who had fought bravely in 1940 and developed a whole theory of offensive tank warfare. Churchill alludes to the poor military performance of France in 1940 which would account for de Gaulle's manner – he had stood firm while others had failed. Moran was an eye witness, but the point is that Churchill did not always apply this empathy with de Gaulle's position to his dealings with him. The source also points to de Gaulle's haughty manner when he cannot offer much in the way of fighting men as support. There were relatively few Free French forces on the Allied side. The uncompromising side of de Gaulle seen in his walk in the garden in B is amplified in Source C. Though the source is triggered by the British occupation of Madagascar, referred to in A, the thrust is that France is the subject of an Anglo-Saxon conspiracy and that the Free French must form a united front against them. As in 1942 the British and the Americans were fighting against Germany in de Gaulle's interests, this does seem to confirm the view in D. Churchill had done his best to maintain France in 1940, even offering union with Britain. It had been France which had endangered the British forces and forced the evacuation of Dunkirk and during that evacuation substantial numbers of French forces had been saved. The USA had accepted the principle of Europe first when it could have concentrated on the Far East, so to use the Madagascar incident to broadcast hostility to the Anglo Saxons does seem unreasonable.

The main source which puts de Gaulle in a favourable light is his own memoirs in A. Given the lack of evidence that he did represent France and his pride and general demeanour, it seems quite generous of Churchill to make the favourable comments he does at Casablanca. De Gaulle was a heroic and in some ways noble figure, but the balance of evidence is that he was largely responsible for the bad relations with his allies.

This is a strong answer. It is relevant and focused on the question and relates the passages to the key issue in the question. It deploys contextual knowledge to make judgements about the sources and it also considers the provenance of the sources.

The answer deals with all four sources and their link to the question is understood. There is some attempt to consider their provenance and also to apply contextual knowledge to assess them. The conclusion follows from the arguments about the evidence and the question is answered directly.

What makes a good answer?

List the characteristics of a good answer to an AS Part (a) question (see page 7) and to an A-level answer using the example and comments above.

Exam Focus (AS question)

REVISED

The following is an AS-type question on one source (Source B on page 44) and model answer.

Use your knowledge of relations between Churchill and de Gaulle to assess how useful Source B is as evidence for how Churchill viewed de Gaulle.

The source indicates Churchill's admiration for de Gaulle and an understanding of his position might be indicative of a good relationship. De Gaulle was a refugee from his own occupied country yet he consistently claimed to represent the spirit of France. Churchill's admiration for fellow figures who were deeply patriotic and represented the 'spirit' of France and its army and for de Gaulle's willingness to fight as 'the last survivor of that warrior race' is representative of Churchill's ideas of heroism. However, though the source is useful in showing how de Gaulle appealed to Churchill's sense of chivalry and his respect for bravery, it is not useful for understanding Churchill's overall relations with de Gaulle. The view was made in confidence to his doctor during the Casablanca Conference where the Allies were struggling to keep unity between themselves and also between the two hostile and feuding French leaders, de Gaulle of the Free French and Giraud, whom Roosevelt and the Americans favoured as the French leader they could support. With the invasion of France approaching and with unconditional surrender as the aim, it was vital to get unity so de Gaulle's arrogance referred to in the source as he stalks 'with his head in the air' was a matter of major irritation for Churchill.

The source is well grasped in relation to the question.

The provenance is understood and it is put into context.

There was more often tension and disagreement between the two men and the source is not reliable as a guide to relations between the two. These had often been poor and there were stormy disagreements both before and after Churchill's more favourable comments in this source. De Gaulle had never been elected as French representative or leader and had put himself forward as leader of the Free French, so when he demanded that he should be recognised as the French leader and be given resources to lead campaigns, the British were annoyed. A particular problem was the refusal of de Gaulle to work with the Vichy leaders in north Africa, whom he saw as traitors at a time when the Allies wanted to focus their attentions on defeating Germany and not to have to worry about arguments or possible opposition from the French authorities in Algeria and Tunisia. Later, Churchill was very reluctant to let de Gaulle assume any authority in France after the Allied invasion, as this would be politically controversial and could create problems in areas liberated by British and American forces. The source is useful as it derives from Churchill's doctor, to whom he could speak freely and privately, and may show Churchill's emotional reaction and sympathy on this

There is knowledge of other issues affecting the relations of the two men.

particular occasion as opposed to his more explosive reaction to de Gaulle's arrogance on other occasions and his concerns about this dividing the Allies and upsetting relations with Roosevelt. However, as a general guide to Churchill's relations with de Gaulle it is less useful.

There is direct judgement about how useful the source is with some balance.

This is a strong answer which looks at what the source is indicating about the relations, puts it into the context of the time and looks at the nature of the source. There is also knowledge applied to assess the usefulness of the evidence by considering its typicality in relation to disputes and bad feelings not shown. There is understanding that de Gaulle's manner is still somewhat haughty.

Further practice (AS question)

Use your knowledge of Churchill's relations with Stalin to assess how useful the following source is for how Churchill viewed Stalin.

SOURCE E

Churchill praises Stalin in an after-dinner speech during the Yalta Conference, February 1945 I walk through the world with greater courage and hope when I find myself in a relation of friendship and intimacy with this great man. Before us lies the realisation of the dream of the poor – that they shall live in peace protected from aggression and evil. My hope is in the illustrious President of the United States and in Marshal Stalin, in whom we shall find the champions of peace.

4 Conservative domination, 1951–64

Why the Conservatives won the election of 1951

After doing better in the general election of 1950 and reducing Labour's majority, in 1951 the Conservatives won the general election with a majority of 26 seats and remained in office until 1964. Labour actually gained 130,000 more votes overall, so it was not a resounding defeat for them, but in key seats the votes swung to the Conservatives. The result can be explained by looking at Labour weaknesses and also at Conservative strengths.

Labour weaknesses

- Labour had not done as well in the election of 1950 as it had in the landslide victory of 1945. It had a majority of only five seats, so this weakened its morale.
- The party was associated with a policy of **Austerity** as it was forced to cut back on imported goods to encourage exports and to maintain high taxation and rationing to ensure that as many goods as possible were exported.
- The Labour Governments faced problems both at home and aboard. The **Korean War** of 1950 meant that defence spending had risen, putting pressure on the money available for spending at home.
- Defence spending had led to cuts in the National Health Service and the introduction of charges for spectacles, prescriptions and dental care. This in turn led to divisions within the Labour Party.

Conservative strengths

- Compared with 1945, the party had better local organisation and finance and campaigned more strongly.
- The party was united behind opposition to Labour nationalising iron and steel, unlike Labour, which was divided.
- Their promise to build 300,000 houses a year was popular, as Labour had not managed to deal with a post-war housing shortage.

- The Conservative campaign promised freedom from rationing and regulations while keeping the key elements that had been popular since 1945 – the welfare state and full employment policies.
- Churchill was still a much-admired figure and in 1951 he did not make controversial speeches like those that had helped to lose the 1945 election.

Other factors

The electoral system failed to work in Labour's favour as the party won more individual votes but fewer seats than the Conservatives. One important factor here was the decline in popularity of the Liberal party from 2.6 million votes in 1945 to only 750,000 in 1951. Most former Liberal voters turned to the Conservatives, as Labour was too associated with the growth of state control of industry, which traditional Liberals disliked. This particularly impacted on marginal Labour seats from the 1950 election. In addition, the changes in the boundaries of parliamentary constituencies made in 1948 tended to favour the Conservatives. Labour kept its support in densely populated industrial areas but in the suburban seats, the Conservatives did better.

International factors also played a role. In 1945 there had been considerable sympathy for socialism, and admiration for the planning and state control of the USSR. However, by 1951 the Cold War had led the USSR to be seen as the enemy, and the controls and regulations under Labour had meant that ideas of socialism and a powerful state were less popular. This led many to vote Conservative.

Labour had had many achievements in 1945–51, but was divided and had somewhat 'run out of steam'. There were new figures in the Conservatives who could be trusted to keep the gains of the post-war period but to give people more freedom.

Spectrum of significance

Below is the conclusion to an answer on the following question:

Assess the reasons why Labour lost the election of 1951.

Annotate the paragraph below to develop the reason for the judgements made about which factor was most significant.

There were many reasons for the election result of 1951 but the main reason was the frustration of many voters with continuing controls, rationing and restrictions and a desire after years of Austerity to return to more normal domestic life. Though there were other reasons these were less important. The fervour of 1945 was no longer present in 1951 and the election of 1950 had left Labour weak with only a small majority. Labour had made big changes and seemed to have little more to offer. In addition, some of the reforms had disappointed and had not led to the social revolution that some had hoped for in 1945. Churchill remained a popular figure but younger Conservatives made it clear that the gains of 1945–51 would be retained but greater freedom would 'set the people free'.

Turning assertion into argument

Below are a sample exam question and a series of assertions. Read the question and then add a justification to each of the assertions to turn it into an argument.

To what extent do Labour weaknesses account for the Conservative victory in 1951?

Labour was divided over key policies.

_____

_____

Conservative campaign strengths were important in explaining the election result.

_____

_____

The electorate was tired of Austerity measures and controls.

_____

_____

The election of 1950 had already shown the weaknesses of Labour.

_____

_____

The Liberals were weak and many voters thought that the Conservatives rather than Labour had more 'Liberal' ideas.

_____

_____

Social changes and their impact on politics, 1951–64

British society changed considerably between 1951 and 1964. The changes may help to explain why the Conservatives were in office for so long and also why by 1964 the British voters felt that it was time for a change.

The standard of living

The 1950s were a period of relatively full employment. Unemployment rose to a peak for the 1950s of 500,000 only in 1959. This is low by modern standards and also by the standards of the inter-war period. This meant that more households had money to spend and a sense of stability. Prosperity led to social change. This may have led to greater support for the Conservatives who seemed to be delivering prosperity.

The level of **real wages** rose. This means that money wages rose faster than prices. So not only did people seem to have more money in their pockets, they could actually buy more.

Greater prosperity made a difference to the way people lived and to the way they saw themselves in terms of social class. More people were able to afford their own homes. Only 25 per cent of people were home owners in 1951 but 44 per cent were in 1964. There were more homes available as more houses were built. Even renting was made easier by a relaxation of controls in 1957. This increased social stability and reduced discontent, possibly favouring the party in power for most of the period, the Conservatives.

Education

There was an expansion of education, with 6,000 more schools built. The Grammar Schools created by the **Butler Act** of 1944 continued to give a greater chance to children whose parents could not have afforded private education. Poorer children had the chance to enter middle-class occupations while improved education saw the middle class expand. Often Grammar Schools had benefited the middle-class voters who kept the Conservatives in office. However, there was the introduction of Comprehensive education to ensure greater fairness and opportunity to school-age children as a whole, many of whom were disadvantaged by an 11+ examination which often favoured more middle-class families. University education was also increased. The state was generous to those going on to higher education and education policies won many votes.

Expectations

The growth of credit and affluence led to changes in what people expected compared with the harder world of the 1920s and 1930s. Homes were more comfortable and housework easier with new domestic appliances. There was a more diverse diet for many people. There were more foreign holidays than ever before, more cars on the roads and better roads. Thus British society became more mobile. Ambitions were more likely to be realised and Britain became recognisably more modern. All this helped the Conservatives to increase their support.

Young people

A more distinct teenage culture emerged. Specific groups like the '**Teddy Boys**' and later the '**Mods and Rockers**' increased the gap between the generations. A responsive manufacturing section realised that young people were consumers and music, clothing and entertainment were produced for a younger market. By 1964, the feeling that Britain was somehow a younger and more vibrant society may have had an impact on the move away from Conservative leaders, who were seen as 'old fashioned'.

Multi-cultural Britain

The influx of immigrants from the West Indies and other parts of the former Empire had an impact on Britain and was to be one of the most significant elements of social change in British history.

By 1964, despite all the social changes that had benefited British society and helped to keep the Conservatives in power, the emergence of a younger, less respectful, more affluent electorate led to a movement for more modernisation, which Labour seemed to represent.

Spot the mistake

Below are a sample exam question and the first paragraph of an answer. Why is this not likely to lead to a high mark? Once you have identified why, rewrite the paragraph.

How important were social changes in explaining why the Conservatives remained in office for so long 1951–64.

The Conservatives remained in office from 1951 to 1964 for many reasons. There were different leaders and they made a different appeal to the people. Labour in the period did not appear united enough to take power. There was also a lot of social change, for example the economy did well and Britain grew. All these reasons help to explain the Conservatives election victories, but the key reason was the weakness of the opposition.

Simple essay style

Below is a sample essay question. Use your own knowledge, information on the opposite page and information from other sections of the book to produce a plan for the question. Choose four general points, and provide three specific pieces of information to support each general point. Once you have planned your essay, write the introduction and conclusion for the essay. The introduction should list the points to be discussed in the essay. The conclusion should summarise the key points and justify your argument.

How far do social changes explain Labour's election victory in 1964?

Conservative economic policies, 1951–64

REVISED

The Conservatives had already in the 1930s accepted a certain amount of government intervention in the economy. After 1951, apart from denationalising iron and steel, they accepted that:

- Britain had some industry run by the state;
- there should not be economic cuts in welfare and health spending;
- it was important to maintain full employment

R.A. Butler and 'Butskellism'

Richard Austen Butler was Chancellor of the Exchequer 1951–55. His policies were similar to those of the Labour leader **Hugh Gaitskell**, hence the term 'Butskellism' to indicate there was little difference between the parties.

'Stop-go'

Butler and his successors have been accused of a policy of 'stop-go'. This meant that if the economy needed to be boosted, then governments would lower interest rates and reduce taxation. This would mean that there was more money to spend and so production for home demand would go up. Chancellors also could increase import duties on imported goods to protect British producers.

If the economy grew too much and prices started to rise (inflation) they would increase interest rates and taxation, especially purchase tax on sales. This would then take money out of the economy and prices would fall.

Successes

- There was a high level of employment for most of the period.
- The economy supported a growth in welfare spending and house building.
- Some industries such as aircraft manufacture, cars and chemicals expanded.
- There was more credit available to help people achieve a higher standard of living. This also helped manufacturers produce goods for the home market such as vacuum cleaners and cars.
- There was some growth in infrastructure as new roads were built and the motorway system began.
- The growth of road transport was developed enough to allow a controversial reduction of the rail network in 1963 as a result of the Beeching Report, which was seen at the time as a major piece of modernisation to save money and cut back loss-making lines, but subsequently came to be criticised as being short-sighted.

Failures

- Britain's rate of economic growth lagged behind that of other countries in Europe.
- Its share of world trade fell. Britain's export markets lagged behind domestic manufacture.
- A lot of money went into defence expenditure (ten per cent of **GDP**, the annual total value of goods and services) rather than into economic improvement.
- There was a failure to modernise traditional industries such as coal and engineering.
- Management methods were often old-fashioned and Britain's economy was high cost and quite labour intensive – trade union influence kept a lot of workplaces overmanned and uneconomical.
- Britain did not join the **European Economic Community (EEC)** and did not benefit from the expansion of the European economy.
- Britain suffered due to persistent price rises (inflation) and lack of modernisation (stagnation).
- From 1961 the economy showed signs of weakness with a rise in unemployment to 800,000 in 1963, worsening labour relations and exports lagged behind imports, and there was a **balance of payments deficit**.

Support or challenge?

Below is a sample exam question which asks whether you agree with a specific statement. Using your knowledge and the information opposite decide whether these statements support or challenge the question and tick the appropriate box.

'The Conservatives failed to deal with Britain's economic needs between 1951 and 1964.' How far do you agree?

Statement	Support	Challenge
1 Britain did not join the European Economic Community.		
2 From 1961 there was higher unemployment.		
3 Unemployment in the 1950s never rose above 500,000 and was lower than in the 1930s.		
4 Governments pursued a 'stop-go' policy of raising interest rates and taxes when prices rose too quickly and reducing them when the economy needed stimulation.		
5 Britain's share of world trade fell in the period 1951–64.		
6 Contemporaries talked of 'stagflation' by the early 1960s.		
7 Governments initiated a greater level of house building in the 1950s than in the 1940s.		
8 In 1963 there were reductions in the railway network as a result of the Beeching Report.		

Introducing an argument

Below are a sample exam question and an introduction. Rewrite the introduction in order to set out an argument that looks at more than one point of view.

How successfully did the Conservatives deal with the economy 1951–64?

The Conservatives were very successful in dealing with the economy and that is why they were successful in three elections. The level of employment remained high and there were far more jobs than there had been in the 1930s. This was because the Tories accepted the need to maintain full employment. There was also the growth of infrastructure with more roads, so much so that railways could be rationalised in 1963 and money saved. The economy was helped by more consumer spending and there was a great deal of house building that put money into the economy.

Conservative leadership

For much of the period the Conservative dominance was helped by its leadership, but by 1964 this had ceased to be the case. Expectations had changed by 1964.

Churchill as peacetime Prime Minister, 1951–55

Churchill had a great reputation as a wartime leader and was respected for his knowledge of foreign affairs. However, his interest in domestic policy was much less strong. At 77 he lacked the energy to offer much in the way of strong leadership and domestic affairs were dominated by R.A. ('Rab') Butler. Churchill suffered a stroke in 1953 which was kept secret and the government continued anyway.

Eden, 1955–57

By 1955, Churchill had to hand over leadership to **Anthony Eden**, who had been waiting in the wings for some time. Eden was a very charming and personable figure, reassuring in manner and highly experienced. But in 1956 he made a very bad policy decision.

Eden and Suez

In anger at the decision of the Egyptian President, Nasser, to nationalise the Suez Canal in 1956, Eden formed a pact with France and Israel and ordered an invasion.

- Eden seemed to be living in the past by worrying about links to the British empire 'East of Suez' and by seeing Nasser as another Hitler.
- Nasser blocked the canal as soon as the invasion began so Britain could not get oil tankers through.
- The USA disapproved of the invasion and had not been consulted.
- The Russians were very hostile to the operation.
- Much British public opinion was very opposed to the invasion.

Eden, normally cautious, had acted recklessly; he was forced to withdraw forces and he resigned in 1957.

Macmillan, 1957–1963

Harold Macmillan did not look and sound too dissimilar to Eden. He faced a disastrous situation with Britain shown to be both foolish and weak as a result of the events in the Suez Canal but his calm leadership made him popular both at home and abroad. He had a distinctive style and unlike Churchill and Eden he was warm and witty, a natural television performer. Despite looking like an Edwardian gentleman and enjoying grouse shooting, he was prepared to move with the times.

With Butler as Home Secretary he moved towards ending the death penalty, national service was ended in 1959 and he made it clear that Britain would have to accept African independence in 1960.

The 1959 election was a high point because Britain seemed very prosperous; Macmillan declared its people had 'never had it so good'. Britain had restored good relations with the USA and Macmillan did his best to build bridges with the USSR.

'A good butcher'

Macmillan was not afraid of making changes. In 1962, he presided over one of the biggest sackings of cabinet ministers in political history when seven senior ministers and nine others lost their jobs.

- Things were not totally positive, however. After 1961, Macmillan was not able to prevent growing economic problems.
- Britain was not playing a very significant part in major world events; for example, the USSR building a wall to divide East and West Berlin and the **Cuban Missile Crisis** of 1962.
- There was a major scandal involving a senior figure, John Profumo, the Defence Minister, compromised by his relationship with an alleged sex worker who had also had relations with the Soviet military attaché.

Macmillan retired in 1963.

Home, 1963–64

Sir Alec Douglas-Home was a Scottish lord who had served with Neville Chamberlain as Lord Dunglass but had given up his peerage. A charming but very obviously aristocratic Old Etonian, Home did not seem at ease in the world of complex economics and challenging foreign affairs problems. He had been chosen not by the party as a whole or even by its MPs but by a small group of senior Conservatives. Home was mercilessly satirised, for instance in the new magazine Private Eye and by satire programmes on TV. He was in power for just under a year as Labour won the 1964 general election.

! Delete as applicable

Below are a sample question and a paragraph written in answer to this question. Read the paragraph and decide which of the possible options (in bold) is most appropriate. Delete the least appropriate options and complete the paragraph by justifying your selection.

Assess the view that Macmillan was the most successful of the Conservative leaders in the period 1951 to 1964.

Macmillan was the most successful leader to a **limited/fair/great extent**. He was a **skilled/reasonable/uneven** communicator in his television broadcasts and his ability to produce memorable phrases. He was a more able leader than **all/some** of the other Conservative premiers. He also was more in tune with the needs of the country and **rather/a great deal/in some ways** more prepared to make changes. He made **limited/some/major** changes to his government when he thought it was necessary. He made a **minor/quite important/very** significant speech on change in Africa and his comment 'You've never had it so good' was highly **uninteresting/insignificant/effective**.

⸙ Identify an argument

Below are a series of definitions, a sample exam question and two sample conclusions. One of the conclusions achieves a high level because it contains an argument. The other achieves a lower level because it contains only description and assertion. Identify which is which. The mark scheme on page 7 will help you.

- Description: a detailed account.
- Assertion: a statement of fact or an opinion, which is not supported by a reason.
- Reason: a statement that explains or justifies something.
- Argument: an assertion justified with a reason.

How far was Conservative domination from 1951–64 the result of strong leadership?

Sample 1

Though leadership did play a part in the Conservative's political domination from 1951 to 1964, this was not the major reason. Churchill had enjoyed a good reputation prior to 1951 but was too old and unwell to be a major influence and his government was dominated by younger figures. Eden, though a suave personality, was seriously compromised by Suez. Macmillan was a well-liked figure but his popularity waned towards the end of his time in office because of growing economic problems and Home was considered out of touch and weak on major economic issues. Thus the key elements were the economic prosperity and, until the 1960s, the lack of a viable alternative.

Sample 2

There were four leaders in this period, Churchill, Eden, Macmillan and Home. Conservative policies moved away in part from Labour's emphasis on controls and state ownership but kept some popular policies like welfare and full employment and also offered more housing. Not all of their policies were popular but Labour could not always take advantage of this and so to an extent it was strong leadership that kept the Tories in power.

Labour in opposition

Labour was in opposition from 1951 to 1964. Was this the result of its own weakness and inability to modernise its appeal to a changing electorate? Was Labour too divided to offer a strong alternative? When Labour did break through in 1964, what had changed?

Lack of unity

Splits in the movement weakened the party.

Broad principles

The leader from 1955, Hugh Gaitskell, wanted to modernise the party, which was still committed to a socialist programme, even though this was obviously less popular than had been the case in 1945.

There was a strong left-wing element in the party led by the former Minister of Health, Aneurin Bevan, who wanted to extend the welfare state, public ownership of industry and redistribution of wealth.

Nationalisation of industry

Bevan argued that Clause IV of the 1918 party constitution should still be a major policy. This was a major part of Labour's programme advocating public ownership of major industries and its most obviously 'socialist' principle. Bevan made a famous speech in 1952, 'In Place of Fear' advocating public ownership of industry. Other elements in the party argued that this was now outdated.

Nuclear disarmament

Many in the party disliked Britain having nuclear weapons for moral reasons and also because of costs. They argued that it took money from social reforms and encouraged a dangerous arms race between the West and the USSR. Others thought that Britain could not be defenceless in a world where the USA and the USSR had nuclear weapons. In 1960, the party voted for unilateral **disarmament** as official policy, though this was later reversed.

Foreign policy

Bevan and the left of the party disapproved of Britain's policy towards West Germany, which had been allowed to rearm and join **NATO**. This was rejected by the leadership and Bevan was expelled in 1955.

Other reasons for Labour's electoral failures in 1955 and 1959

- **Clement Attlee** did not appear to be as robust as Eden in the electoral campaign in 1955 and seemed tired and unwell.
- The party had a negative attitude to joining Europe, which made them seem isolationist and old-fashioned, given the EEC's high growth rates.

- Hugh Gaitskell, the moderate Labour leader, was not seen as being able to wield authority over a divided party.
- During the 1959 election campaign, Labour made unconvincing statements about being able to raise social spending, for example on pensions, without raising taxes.
- In 1959 13.7 million voted Conservative and 12.5 million voted Labour. There were only 1.6 million Liberal votes, a decline from the ten per cent who voted Liberal in 1945. Most of these votes went to the Conservatives.

Is it fair to blame Labour for the defeats?

Blame can be attributed to Labour as their election campaigns in 1955 and 1959 were not well managed. Their policies seemed little different from the Conservatives', who had accepted popular ideas like the welfare state and promoting high employment. The left of the party was promoting policies which were popular in industrial areas but less appealing to the growing middle classes. Labour also failed to take advantage of the unpopularity of the Conservatives over the Suez Crisis.

However, other factors were also important:
- The Conservatives offered attractive low-tax policies.
- Until 1961, the Conservatives were helped by a period of economic prosperity.
- Macmillan's personality and his ability to find strong phrases captured the public's support.
- The gap in the popular vote between Conservative and Labour was not so great as the number of seats – in 1959 only 1.5 million more people voted for the Conservatives but they won 107 more seats.

What does the victory of 1964 show about Labour's performance before that?

The election victory of 1964 shows that Labour won more support when:
- a younger and more classless leader emerged
- Labour looked more to the future and argued for modernisation and technological change
- divisions were less obvious.

However, by 1964 there was less prosperity and less effective leadership on the Conservative side.

Complete the paragraph

Below are a sample exam question and a paragraph written in answer to the question. The paragraph lacks a clear point at the start, but does contain supporting material and an explanatory link back to the question at the end. Complete the paragraph by writing in the key point at the start. Use the space provided.

To what extent was Labour responsible for its failure to gain office from 1951 to 1964?

_____

_____

This point is supported by the divisions within the party. These had begun before 1951 with criticisms by Labour's left of the introduction of prescription charges. Many were also unhappy about the foreign policy and the links with the USA. There were ongoing divisions about the support of German rearmament and the maintenance of Britain's independent nuclear deterrent. The left of the party was unwilling to abandon the policy of nationalisation and public ownership even when it was clear that there was little public interest in it and that existing nationalised industries were not being run on a socialist model. However, the ability of the Conservatives to win over the middle ground and the decline of the Liberal vote were equally important. Thus the explanation cannot be totally one-sided.

Mind map

Use the information on the opposite page and your own knowledge to add detail to the mind map below to identify some of the weaknesses of Labour in 1951–64.

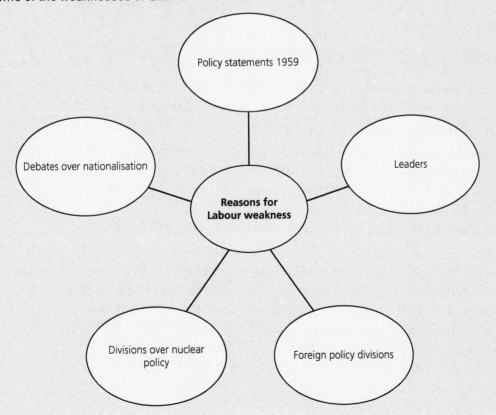

Exam focus

Below is a sample high level answer to a Section B exam-style question. Read the answer and the comments around it.

How far was the Conservative domination between 1951 and 1964 a result of the weakness of the Labour opposition?

The Conservative domination resulted from their success in three successive elections. Some of the success was due to the prosperity which Britain enjoyed in the 1950s and to the popularity of Conservative policies and leaders. However, the main reason was the failure of Labour to provide an effective opposition, especially as the decline of the Liberals meant that many of the middle-class votes in marginal constituencies went to the Conservatives, as voters disliked some key Labour policies which remained popular in Labour's heartland.

> This paragraph sets out a clear view and introduces some possible explanations. It is well focused on the question.

Labour had left office in 1951 a divided party, with many on the left being disappointed with the reforms passed after the war, the support for the USA in foreign policy and the restrictions on spending which resulted in cuts to the NHS and prescription charges. These divisions continued and prevented Labour from taking advantage of some considerable Conservative weaknesses.

The Conservatives lacked a modern, dynamic leader as Churchill was obviously too old and unwell in his return to the premiership. The Suez Crisis was unpopular in 1956, yet they still won the 1959 election. There were criticisms of the management of the economy. But Labour was not really able to exploit these until 1964.

Labour could not agree on the future of socialism. The electorate had voted for the easing of economic restrictions and the belief in state planning and nationalisation of industries was much less than it had been immediately after the war. However, the left wing of Labour persisted in its belief in what Bevan called in his 1952 speech 'In Place of Fear' 'the substitution of public for private ownership'. The Clause IV of the Labour constitution of 1918 continued to divide the party.

Perhaps more significant was the division over nuclear policy and foreign policy. On nuclear policy the divisions were more complex, with Bevan actually supporting a nuclear deterrent which divided him from many on the left who rejected it. However, Bevan was at odds with the right of the party over issues of foreign policy such as the rearming of West Germany. In 1960, Gaitskell was forced by a party vote to accept unilateral disarmament as a policy.

> There is clear and developed explanation of the key issue in the question. It is always best to start with the factor in the question.

Fears of a radical left was only one of the reasons for Labour's poor performance. The other was that their official policies did not appear to be offering anything very different from the Conservatives, who had accepted many of the post-war policies on employment and welfare. Thus there was the phrase 'Butskellism' to describe a similar approach taken by the Conservative Chancellor Butler and his Labour counterpart and future leader Hugh Gaitskell.

However, Labour weakness alone could not have explained the Conservative domination. The number of votes cast was not radically different between the parties. In 1959, 13.7 million voted Conservative and 12.5 million voted Labour. Only 1.6 million people voted for the Liberals. Thus the Liberals who had got ten per cent of the vote in 1945 had declined considerably and it was the Conservatives who were more successful in picking up their votes. Labour maintained its support in traditional Labour areas but did not manage to widen its appeal. This was partly because of divisions and some poor campaigning. In 1959, for instance, they did not properly explain how they would raise pensions without increasing taxes. The Conservatives seemed more financially and economically competent.

> This paragraph deals with 'How far' and takes the answer away from a list of factors.

The 1950s were a period of relatively high employment and growing consumer prosperity. There was more house-building and an end to the rationing which had continued in the post-war period under Labour. The Conservatives capitalised on the prosperity, encouraging purchasing on credit, encouraging more road use and creating mini booms by their fiscal and interest rate policies. Macmillan struck a chord in 1959 when he told the public that they had never had it so good, and Labour found it difficult to compete. Social change tended to favour the Conservatives, too, with suburban growth, the development of a larger middle class, more home ownership and social mobility.

There are some good links here between the different factors.

When economic prosperity began to falter in the early 1960s and Conservative leadership seemed less effective, with scandals like the Profumo affair, then Labour was able to gain more support. However, this needed a leader, Harold Wilson, who was able to offer more unity and more distinctive policies of modernisation and technological development. Even so the result was close and it was not until 1966 that Wilson got a working majority.

The argument could be a bit stronger here.

Obviously, Conservative strengths and that party's ability to exploit the changing economic and social conditions after 1951 are important, but more crucial is Labour's failure to attract key voters and to offer a more united front. When it seemed more unified and with more modern policies it succeeded.

There is a view offered here though it might have been more developed.

This is a really strong answer. It offers analysis, i.e. it links material to the question. It would reach the higher levels because it goes beyond listing factors and offers some judgement about their relative importance. The points it makes go beyond assertions and there is some well-chosen evidence used in support.

Exam focus activity

In order to reach the very top level, candidates need to reach judgements about the issues they are considering in relation to the question. Identify paragraphs where the candidate has done this successfully and those where a judgement is either absent or not developed. In the latter case write a couple of sentences for each of the paragraphs so that a judgement based on the argument is reached.

Why did the Conservatives lose the election of 1964?

The 1964 election was not a landslide victory like that of 1945. Labour actually gained fewer votes than in 1959, but the Conservatives lost 1.6 million votes and the Liberals gained over 1.5 million votes. Thus, it may have been more a question of discontented middle-class voters going to the Liberals rather than a big swing to Labour.

Possible reasons for the result

The loss of popularity by the Conservatives

The Conservative's leader, Sir Alec Douglas-Home, seemed out of touch with the modern electorate. However, this can be overstated. Many people found Douglas-Home to be more trustworthy than Labour's leader, **Harold Wilson**. Many blamed the Conservative's economic record. There were accusations that Britain had had '13 wasted years' and had fallen behind other countries, and there was much talk of inflation, unemployment and decline in manufacturing areas. In reality, the Conservatives had cut income tax in 1963 and the number out of work fell. The Tories had had a bad press over the Profumo scandal (see page 54), which was seen as an upper class sex scandal, but this did not appear to have a huge impact on traditional Tory supporters: older voters and women who were interviewed in opinion polls continued to prefer the Conservatives.

The appeal of Labour

The new Labour leader, Harold Wilson, was seen as a man of the people who offered a break from the public school–educated political leaders since 1945. His appeal can be exaggerated though as Wilson, though articulate, was not a charismatic leader like **Tony Blair** later on. It was certainly true that Labour stopped quarrelling so much in public and seemed more united, though few of the team had experience in government. Wilson made an appeal to those who wanted a more modern, scientific and technological Britain by appealing for economic planning and using the technological revolution to take Britain forward. However, it was not entirely clear what Wilson meant by 'technological revolution'! Labour's campaign was broader in its appeal and more carefully targeted than in the past. For example, the party's election manifesto offered social progress, but did not stress nationalisation of industry as this was not popular.

Labour did not actually gain all that many more votes. Many voters were concerned with Labour's left wing and the influence of trade unions. In some areas Labour lost votes because voters disliked immigration and thought the Tories were more likely to control it.

Other factors

There were other reasons for Labour's victory. Many felt that after 13 years it was just time for a change. This was particularly true of younger votes who had known only Conservative rule, though few younger voters actually turned out to vote. There had been considerable changes in Britain since 1951. There had been excitement about technology; space exploration; more opportunities to travel; more educational opportunities. The world seemed to be changing rapidly and Labour seemed more in tune with a new society than the Tories.

Another important factor was something of a revival for the Liberals. Relatively few voters switched from Conservative to Labour; more decided to vote Liberal. Though the Liberals won only three more seats than in 1959, the split in some marginal constituencies between Conservatives and Liberals was significant in bringing about Labour victories in constituencies which they had not taken in 1959.

The growth of satire on TV and in the press and a less respectful attitude to politicians was another factor. Satirists poked fun at Wilson for his lower-middle-class habits and manners – he was supposed to like HP sauce and the attempts at poetry by his wife Mary were the subject of some unkind mockery. Generally, though, satire mocked the Conservatives and therefore seemed to benefit Labour.

Spectrum of importance

Below are a sample exam question and a list of general points which could be used to answer it. Use your knowledge and the information on the page opposite to reach a judgement about the relative importance of the factors (that is what 'assess' means) Write numbers on the spectrum below to indicate their relative importance. Having done this, write a brief justification of your placement on the line, explaining why some of these factors are more important than others. The resulting diagram could form the basis of an essay plan.

Assess the reasons why Labour won the election of 1964.

1   Economic downturn

2   A new leader

3   Douglas-Home's leadership

4   Scandals affecting the Conservatives

5   The Liberal revival

6   Labour more united

Least important ←————————————————————————→ Most important

Eliminate irrelevance a

Below are a sample exam question and a paragraph written in answer to the question. Read the paragraph and identify the parts of the paragraph that are not directly relevant to the question. Draw a line through the information that is irrelevant and justify your deletions in the margin.

To what extent was Labour's victory in 1964 due to Harold Wilson?

Harold Wilson offered a more focused and dynamic leadership and he stressed the need for Britain to become more modern, scientific and technological. In 1950 Wilson had been a member of Attlee's Government when there had been a dispute about prescription charges and he had resigned. Wilson's premiership did not always put into practice what the Prime Minister had promised and he found that economic problems were often too difficult to allow reforms. Wilson's leadership was able to unify Labour more, and this was a major reason for victory. Wilson also seemed more modern and realistic than his rival, Douglas-Home. Wilson made use of the public's concern about Britain's lack of competitiveness. Later, though, he was unable to deal with some of the same problems, particularly inflation.

Wilson's Governments, 1964–70

In 1964, Wilson had a majority of only four MPs. Given that divisions in the party had not gone away, Wilson did well to increase his majority in 1966, winning 100 seats more than the Conservatives. However, in 1970, Wilson lost the election and many in his own party were disappointed at his lack of progress.

What problems did Wilson face in 1964?

Wilson faced many problems when he became Prime Minister in 1964. Stagflation characterised the economy and there were other economic issues. Britain's growth was very slow compared to other developed industrial countries, nationalised industries were very costly due to a lack of investment in the 1950s and defence costs were very high and prevented domestic investment. Away from the economy, changes in society had not been reflected in the existing laws and the education system did not offer enough high quality technical and scientific training or widespread opportunities for students to go into higher education.

What did Wilson achieve?

Social reforms

Roy Jenkins as Home Secretary undertook a policy of modernisation that led to some of the most significant domestic changes in the century.

- Race relations laws made discrimination illegal.
- The voting age was lowered from 21 to 18.
- Capital punishment was ended.
- The equal pay law meant men and women had to receive the same pay for the same work.
- Abortion was legalised and more contraception was made available.
- Sexual acts between consenting adults of the same sex in private were legalised.

Education

For schools, the Comprehensive system was expanded. In higher education, the Open University was established to give greater access to higher education to people of all ages and the number of universities increased following the advice of the 1963 Robbins Report on Higher Education.

Economic policy

There were some positive economic developments. The balance of payments deficit was improving by 1969 and the value of sterling had been maintained to the benefit of Britain's very important financial sector. The Government encouraged industrial developments in key areas in south Wales and Merseyside and there were developments in road transport as motorways were built in the north.

What did Wilson fail to achieve?

The economy

Economic problems continued throughout the period and forced the Government to abandon several manifesto policies, such as reintroducing free prescription charges and raising the school leaving age. There were ongoing problems with the balance of payments deficit and rising prices, which forced the Government into introducing unpopular spending cuts and higher taxes. Unemployment remained a problem for much of the period of Labour's rule. By 1967 it was at a post-war high of 2.5 million. Another sign of lack of economic progress was when Britain was forced to devalue the pound in 1967 because of a lack of overseas confidence in the economy.

Many economic policies failed to deliver positive results. Investment did not lead to much-needed modernisation and attempts at economic planning in the National Plan and the new Department of Economic affairs achieved little. Failure to join the EEC meant that Britain still did not benefit from the rapidly growing trade in Europe.

Trade unions

Labour was traditionally the party of organised labour, but had to try to bring in reforms.

- There was a plan for long-term reform in 1967 when a leading Minister Barbara Castle introduced a proposal 'In Place of Strife'. This would require unions to ballot members before calling strikes, and also try to achieve settlements by arbitration. This plan was so unpopular among the Labour left, the trade unions and some cabinet ministers that it was abandoned.
- Strikes caused major problems. A seamen's strike in 1966 damaged the economy and led to the loss of confidence which brought about devaluation.
- Economic growth was hampered by high costs brought about by some union practices which encouraged overmanning in manufacturing industry.
- Trade union membership actually fell because of the decline of traditional manufacturing.

Wilson made Labour once more a party of government after a long period in opposition, and did modernise many aspects of Britain; but economic problems were harder to deal with, and the position of trade unions remained an unresolved issue.

You're the examiner

Below are a sample exam question and a paragraph written in answer to this question. Read the paragraph and the mark scheme provided on page 7. Decide which level you would award the paragraph. Write the level below along with a justification for your decision.

How successfully did Labour deal with the problems it faced between 1964 and 1970?

Labour faced considerable problems because of a build-up of economic problems and social change which had not all been addressed by Conservative Governments and also because of long-term lack of growth, investment and modernisation. Labour faced both short-term and longer-term problems requiring changes in education, industrial relations and a lack of competitiveness. Wilson also faced a difficult initial period with a small parliamentary majority. In many ways he was successful politically in that he turned this majority into a larger victory in the 1966 election, showing that he had gained more trust in Labour. He also produced distinctive policies for economic planning with the National Plan and for reforms in industrial relations. He kept his party together in difficult times and achieved reforms in education and also in bringing the law up to date to reflect a changing society. Some key changes in the law relating to gay and lesbian people and abortion were made and there was a very important expansion of education in the creation of the Open University. However, in the short term he was less successful, damaging his reputation by the devaluation of 1967, not being able to deal effectively with 'stagflation' or to control the trade unions with the 'In Place of Strife' white paper. The belief in planning and control of wages and prices showed problems of governing Britain that were not unique to Labour and bold initiatives that were theoretically valuable did not always work in practice.

Level:

_____

Reason for choosing that level:

_____

_____

Recommended reading

- Andrew Marr, *A History of Modern Britain*, pages 231–312 (2009)
- Mike Wells and Nick Fellows, *Britain, 1930–1997*, pages 111–26 (2015)
- Alan Sked and Chris Cook, *Post-War Britain*, pages 200–52 (1993)
- M Lynch, *Britain 1945–2007*, pages 81–93 and 102–9 (2015)

5 Labour and Conservative Governments, 1964–79

The 1970 election

Labour was expected to win the 1970 election but the Conservatives under their leader **Edward Heath** gained 43 more seats. A striking element was the loss of nearly a million Labour votes since 1966. In 1966, many felt that Labour should be given a chance and had shown clear modernising trends. By 1970, it was clear that Labour's record had been patchy and that long-term problems of competitiveness had not really been addressed. Britain's industries had too many old-fashioned practices and could not compete in terms of productivity or cost with their overseas rivals.

Divisions within the Labour movement

Splits in the Labour Party had re-emerged. The need for cuts in spending had felt like betrayal to many Labour supporters. The left accused the leaders of maintaining the needs of the financial sector at the expense of the ordinary people and of manufacturing. Many in the left of the party disliked the diplomatic support that Wilson had given to the USA in its war against the Communists in North Vietnam. The trade unions – a key element in Labour's history and in the party as a whole – disliked the proposals to restrict union power.

Party membership had fallen and Labour had seemed to lack idealism and commitment to its own roots of working people.

Economic problems

- Economic planning efforts had not yielded much and unemployment was higher in 1970 than it had been when Labour took office.
- The Government had not controlled inflation and retail prices had risen by 33 per cent.
- There had been a fall in employment in mining and manufacturing – two areas where Labour had been expected to defend the interests of working people.
- Wilson had been accused of lying when he said that the devaluation of the pound in 1967 would not affect 'the pound in your pocket' as it did lead to higher prices for imported goods.

The appeal of the Conservatives

Edward Heath was, like Wilson, a Grammar school–educated leader, not one of the Tory public school elite. He seemed a modern figure and did not tolerate old-fashioned, racist ideas, as was shown when he sacked the right-wing politician Enoch Powell for an anti-immigration speech from the shadow cabinet in 1968. Heath had very clear policies which appealed to many middle-class voters and also was passionate about joining the EEC, which many saw as essential for Britain's economic future now that the Commonwealth was so much less important.

By 1970, the gap between the ideologies of the parties had grown since the days of Butskellism. Heath was proposing less government intervention in the economy, and fewer attempts to control wages and prices directly. Many tax payers disagreed with Wilson's policies of maintaining certain industries that were obviously inefficient and making a loss. Heath was also able to make the power of the unions a key issue. Many people were worried about the strikes and restrictive practices, which seemed unfair to non-unionised workers and kept costs and prices high. Heath spoke for many suburban middle-class voters who thought Labour had mismanaged the economy and had appeased, rather than confronted, over-powerful unions.

What was the key factor?

Heath was not a charismatic figure, and was rather cold and stilted. Wilson was a better performer on TV. However, it was clear that Labour had been bitterly divided over trade union policy, whereas the Conservatives were united behind Heath's determination to modernise labour relations. Furthermore, Europe was not the divisive issue among the Tories in 1970 that it was to become later in the century and beyond. The Liberal vote fell slightly, so the trend for Liberals to split the vote was not as strong as it had been in 1966. It was claimed that Labour suffered from voter apathy, whereas for Conservatives, the trade union issue gave them a cause.

Complete the paragraph

a

Below are a sample exam question and a paragraph written in answer to the question. The paragraph contains a point and specific examples, but lacks a concluding explanatory link back to the question. Complete the paragraph by adding this link (remember that 'assess' the reasons involves more than explaining some reasons).

Assess the reasons for the Conservative success in the election of 1970.

The election of 1970 was a reflection of concern that Labour could not deal with Britain's underlying problems concerning industrial relations and also that despite efforts to control prices, inflation was still high and unemployment showed little signs of falling. Heath, though not a strong communicator, put forward quite distinctive Conservative policies which appealed to the key marginal voters of middle England and which involved less state interference and more promotion of enterprise and a strong commitment to Europe. The election could be explained both by weaknesses and divisions within Labour and a stronger and more clearly communicated programme by the Tories.

_____

_____

Simple essay style

Below is a sample exam question. Use your own knowledge and information on the opposite page to produce a plan for the question. Choose four or five general points, and provide three pieces of specific information to support each general point. Once you have planned your essay, write the introduction and conclusion for the essay. The introduction should list the points to be discussed in the essay. The conclusion should summarise the key points and justify which point was the most important.

How important was the issue of trade union reform in deciding the result of the election of 1970?

Heath's Government and problems with industrial relations

Heath wanted to unify the nation through better regional development; to improve social services; to join the EEC, which he hoped would increase trade and to modernise industrial relations.

What were the problems Heath faced?

- Inflation proved difficult to control. War in the Middle East in 1973 raised prices.
- In 1971, America changed its policy towards exchange rates and let the dollar fall in value. This meant that British exports were more expensive.
- The Government felt obliged to subsidise some failing industries to protect jobs.
- Entering the EEC was successful, but Britain had to accept some unfavourable terms.
- The number of working days lost in strikes increased from 10.9 million in 1970 to 23 million in 1972.

Why was industrial relations policy so important?

The issue with trade unions came to be central to the success, or otherwise, of Edward Heath's Government on two fronts. Firstly, from an economic perspective, unless costs were kept competitive, Britain would not benefit from the opportunities opened by entry to the EEC. Also, it was difficult to stop inflation caused by high government spending and external factors, so it was important to try to prevent wage-led inflation. Secondly, Conservatives and their supporters had disapproved of Labour's climb-down over 'In Place of Strife'. They therefore saw it as a sign of political strength to succeed where Wilson had failed. However, the trade unions had become very influential. Their leaders were determined to resist what they saw as class-based restrictions, and some militant trade unionists wanted to bring down the Heath Government.

What was the Government's policy?

In 1971, the Conservative Government introduced the Industrial Relations Act. This ended the so-called closed shop and gave the Government the right to insist on a 60-day cooling off period before a strike was called and to insist that all trade unionists were balloted about a potential strike. In addition, a new Industrial Relations Commission was created to help to negotiate to avoid strikes.

Problems in the coal industry

In January 1972, 280,000 coal miners went on strike. This threatened heating and power supplies for industry. It led to power cuts and a surrender by the Government. The miners had asked for a huge 47 per cent pay increase, and were eventually awarded a pay rise higher than the inflation rate.

This was important because:

- it weakened any government strategy to reduce inflation
- it showed the power of the miners and the effectiveness of their methods
- it showed how alarmed the Government was about threatening picketing action and the use of 'flying pickets' (groups of miners who travelled from pit to pit to support the local miners who were on strike)
- many Conservatives saw the rule of law being challenged
- other workers followed the miners in making wage claims.

The clash of 1973

By November, the **oil crisis** had led to much higher price rises. The miners began an overtime ban. Heath had several options:

1. To accept the wage rises and risk making inflation even worse.
2. To leave the negotiations to the National Coal Board and risk another strike threatening power and bringing industries to a standstill and people cold in their homes.
3. To introduce emergency powers.

Heath went with the third option:

- Industry and businesses could have access to electricity for only three days a week.
- To cut down on petrol, there was a 50 mph limit for all cars.
- TV was ordered to stop broadcasting at 10.30 to save electricity.

Heath decided to get a mandate for these measures and to force through industrial relations reform by holding an election. But there was little to choose between the votes for the two major parties. Labour got four more seats than the Conservatives.

i The flaw in the argument a

Below is a sample exam question and part of an answer to it. Identify the flaw in the argument and suggest how the answer could be improved. Write your answers below.

'The achievements of the Heath Government between 1970 and 1974 were limited.' How far do you agree?

The Government of Edward Heath achieved little because of the confrontation with the miners, which caused him to call an election on the issue of who governs Britain. This was a fundamental political mistake as the voters did not respond to his calls for solidarity against the unions and Labour was voted back into power. The emergency measures, which Heath took, threw Britain into a state of crisis and showed the power of the unions rather than the ability of the Government to deal with a crisis. Thus Heath showed that he could not really deal with industrial relations any more successfully than Wilson had in the failed 'In Place of Strife' initiative and together with Heath's awkward manner and his failure to communicate effectively confirmed that little could be achieved by the Conservative Government.

The flaw is:

_____

The paragraph could be improved by:

_____

_____

i Turning assertion into argument

Below are a sample exam question and a series of assertions. Read the question and then add a justification to each of the assertions to turn it into an argument.

How successful was the Government of Edward Heath, 1970–74, in dealing with the problems that it faced?

Heath was successful in Europe.

_____

_____

Heath had to make some policy U-turns which made him appear unsuccessful.

_____

_____

Heath was unsuccessful in dealing with the problem of strikes.

_____

_____

Wilson and Callaghan, 1974–79

Why did Labour win in February 1974?

Labour's win in the first election of 1974 can, to some extent, be explained by Conservative failures. Many voters disliked the choice offered in the Conservative question 'Who Governs Britain?'. Heath seemed to have lost control of the country, and did not communicate effectively. Even those who disapproved of the miners' actions were themselves facing higher prices which caused discontent, and many thought the Three-Day Week over-dramatic. On other policies, some former Conservative voters disliked the terms of entry into Europe, which involved losing the cheap food from the Commonwealth and subsidising Europe's farmers through the unpopular Common Agricultural Policy.

Wilson's more conciliatory line was accepted. But he was not overwhelmingly popular. Another election in October saw Labour win fewer votes, but it did get an overall majority of three and won 318 seats to the Tories' 277.

The problems of the Labour government 1974–79

Splits in the Labour movement and relations with the trade unions again caused problems. There were divisions between left and right factions of the party as two influential left wingers – Michael Foot and Tony Benn – joined the cabinet and clashed with Labour's more moderate leaders. The party was also divided over entry to the EEC and Wilson had to hold a referendum in 1975, which the 'stay' side won. As legislation had failed, Labour had to get agreement with the trade unions and produced the Social Contract. This failed to stop a wave of strikes in 1978–79 (see below).

Labour found it difficult to deal with the trade unions because of the historic links between the unions and the party, which had depended on union support in the early days, and also because unions had 'block votes' at Labour conferences depending on the size of their membership so they therefore could be influential.

The economy was the other major issue. Inflation continued to rise, reaching an average of over 25 per cent a year. The war between Israel and its Arab neighbours in 1973 had led to higher oil prices worldwide. Trade unions responded to higher prices with demands for more pay. Labour accepted a pay rise for miners of 29 per cent, which encouraged other groups to demand more and then had to fall back on making spending cuts to reduce inflation and also to imposing a legal limit on wage increases, which was unpopular. The economy was also seen to be stagnating with low growth rates, low productivity and low investment. Wilson suddenly and unexpectedly resigned because he was fearful that his mental capacities were declining, in March 1976. This led to a lack of confidence in the financial markets and the value of the pound fell. The new leader, James Callaghan, and his Chancellor of the Exchequer, Denis Healey, were forced to make heavy cuts in spending to secure a key loan to support the pound. As the Government became unpopular, Labour was forced into a pact with the 13 Liberal MPs just to stay in power in 1977–78. This led to a lack of confidence in the financial markets.

The winter of discontent, 1978–79

The 'winter of discontent' was some newspapers' name for a series of particularly severe industrial disputes.
- As inflation rose and wages were frozen, the trade unions once again pressed for big wage increases.
- Strikes in the winter of 1978–79 hit key public services such as rubbish collection.
- The press claimed that there was a severe crisis.
- The Government failed to keep its promises to begin devolution for Scotland and Wales, and the Scottish and Welsh nationalist MPs voted against them and brought the Government down in March 1979.

Did Labour deserve to lose the election of 1979?

Labour were not entirely to blame for the problems. Inflation and economic stagnation were inherited and were faced by other countries, like the USA. With regards to industrial relations, the press sensationalised the industrial disputes and strikes, and Labour had been able to co-operate with the unions until the Social Contract broke down under pressure from rising prices. Labour may have broken its promise for devolution, but the voters in Scotland and Wales did not show their support for this in referenda held in March 1979.

However, Labour was deeply divided, and did not offer a solution to increasing strikes. Alongside this, there were no strategies to deal with longer-term problems in the economy. Callaghan did not appear to recognise how serious the situation was by 1979. In the election, Labour could not match the effective campaign waged by the Conservatives under Margaret Thatcher.

Spot the mistake

Below are a sample exam question and a paragraph written in answer to the question. What mistake is stopping the paragraph being of a high quality? Rewrite the paragraph so that it displays the qualities of at least level 5. The mark scheme is on page 7.

'Labour's main weakness from 1974–79 was its failure to deal with industrial relations.' How far do you agree?

> Labour failed to deal with industrial problems and economic difficulties and that meant that it lost much support. However, what brought the government down was the failure to implement devolution measures for Scotland and Wales leading to the Nationalist MPs voting with the Conservatives. The decision of Wilson to stand down had meant that an established leader had to be replaced which may have weakened the government. Labour also lost its temporary alliance with the Liberals and so by 1979 was vulnerable to internal relations with other parties being weak.

Introducing an argument

Below is a sample exam question, a list of key points to be made in the essay, and a simple introduction and conclusion for the essay. Read the question, the key points and the introduction and conclusion. Rewrite the introduction and conclusion in order to develop an argument.

To what extent was the 'winter of discontent' responsible for Labour losing the election of 1979?

Key points:
- The Winter of Discontent saw public services disrupted by strikes.
- There were deep divisions within the Labour Party.
- Inflation was a serious problem.
- Wilson's sudden and unexpected departure from office.
- The strong campaign led by the Conservatives.
- The Scottish and Welsh nationalist MPs were angry because they could not obtain a vote on plans to devolve powers to local assemblies.

Introduction

> There were many reasons why Labour lost the election of 1979. The public faced rising prices and a sense that Britain was falling behind her competitors. There were on going problems with industrial relations and also the sudden departure of Wilson had left the party divided.

Conclusion

> Thus we may see that various factors led to the defeat of Labour after the press was very hostile to Callaghan about the so-called winter of discontent and his failure to recognise the sense of crisis. There were long-term factors as well, which were important.

Exam focus

Below is a sample exam question and model response. Read the answer and the comments around it.

'Industrial relations were the main problem facing governments between 1964 and 1979.'
To what extent do you agree with this view?

Industrial relations became an increasing problem for both Labour and Conservative Governments in this period and were important in leading to electoral defeats in 1970, 1974 and 1979. However, it was more the underlying economic weaknesses and the failure of governments to confront industrial change that were the main problems. ●

> This sets out the 'thesis' of the answer very clearly and addresses the issue of 'to what extent'.

Trade union membership was an important part of British life, with almost half of the workforce in unions in the 1960s. A large number of restrictive practices had grown up which increased costs and lowered productivity. However, unions were also under pressure from rising prices to support their members' standard of living. Labour had to be careful when dealing with trade unions because of their historical links with the party and their block vote in national conferences.

Wilson's ideas for modernisation and effective planning depended on rises in productivity and Britain's economic competitiveness. By the late 1960s, strike threats and demands for higher pay to keep up with inflation were threatening Labour's plans. Unions opposed wage controls, defended the 'closed shop' and were prepared to support strike actions to maintain real wages even at the cost of threatening key supplies and services.

Wilson and one of his leading ministers, Barbara Castle, attempted to introduce union reform to insist on strike ballots and arbitration. However, 'In Place of Strife' was resisted strongly by the unions and many Labour MPs. This caused a considerable problem in dividing the Labour movement. The failure to restrict industrial action meant continuing economic problems and also political problems in that the government appeared weak, and gave the Conservatives a political advantage. ●

> This section could be seen as explanation rather than judgement but is important in explaining the nature of the problems. Note that the answer keeps coming back to 'problems'.

Heath had the political support after the 1970 election to reform industrial relations, but despite compulsory measures establishing an Industrial Relations Commission and compulsory ballots and a cooling-off period, the number of strikes increased from 11 million working days lost in 1970 to 24 million in 1973. The Government was powerless to prevent a successful miners' strike in 1972 and confrontation with the miners again in late 1973 led to considerable problems with shortage of power and a compulsory 'three day week'. It also led to the political problem of an election on 'who governs Britain'. Thus industrial relations seemed to move to the forefront of British politics and be the key issue that actually toppled the Government.

It was important for Labour to avoid further confrontation and they moved away from compulsion and towards a negotiated agreement called the Social Contract. By 1978, however, this proved no more successful than Heath's Industrial Relations Act, and unions abandoned informal deals to restrict wage rises. The so-called 'winter of discontent' in 1978–79 saw a renewal of strikes and disputes, which could be exploited by the Conservatives and played a major role in Labour's defeat in 1979. Thus between 1964 and 1979 industrial relations caused not only economic problems in increasing costs and reducing trade, but they also caused major political problems for both parties. ●

> A distinction is made between economic and political problems.

However, it could be argued that industrial relations were more of a result of other problems than being the main problem. Britain had not maintained high growth rates in comparison with its competitors; it had low productivity because of under-investment. The British economy also suffered from inflation for other reasons than trade union activities, for example from the oil price rise following the Arab–Israeli war in 1973, which affected not just Britain but the USA and the West generally. Trade unions often reacted to rising prices by demanding higher pay and also opposed attempts to maintain financial stability through cuts in spending. For example, the breakdown of the Social Contract owed much to resentment at Healey's economic policies. Thus trade unions were not the major problem faced by governments but rather accumulated economic decline inherited from the 1950s, 'stagflation' and problems in the world economy. Also, trade union problems did arise from political misjudgement. Heath's election strategy, which pitted government against unions, did not meet with general public approval. Callaghan's failure to see the political importance of the Winter of Discontent was as important as the actual problem of strikes. Trade unions were a serious issue but only because of underlying economic problems and some poor political decisions.

> There is a distinct argument here and the factors are linked together.

> The student offers a clear view of the relative importance of trade unions.

This is a good answer but it could be improved if the other factors in the last paragraph were more developed. It is more than a series of explained problems but the bulk of the assessment is at the end and this could be better balanced. The alternative factors need more explanation and support; however, the answer is analytical.

Reverse engineering

The best essays are based on careful plans. Read the essay and the comments and try to work out the general points of the plan used to write the essay. Once you have done this, note down the specific examples used to support each general point and, where examples are either weak or lacking, use this book to help you find precise details.

6 Thatcher and the end of consensus, 1979–97

Why Thatcher won three elections

The election of 1979

Margaret Thatcher was a striking 'conviction politician', with clear views which offered a break with the past at a time when there was much talk of 'decline' and 'the need for modernising Britain'. Labour's overall vote increased in 1979, but the electoral system favoured the Conservatives. Marginal seats were key and Thatcher appealed to marginal voters, especially in London, the Midlands and the south-east by stressing the need for trade union reform and attacking 'socialism'. She also had some key press support. Labour seemed divided and to have no strategy to deal with rising strike actions, inflation, unemployment and economic stagnation (see page 68). The Conservatives also gained support from former Liberal voters, as the Liberals had helped to keep Labour in power 1977–78 and were damaged by Labour's unpopularity over the 'Winter of Discontent'.

The election of 1983

The Conservatives actually polled fewer votes than 1979 in this election, but the Labour vote fell from 11.5 million to 8.5 million, giving Thatcher a convincing majority. This was despite rising unemployment and controversial policies. Her privatisation policies were well underway by 1983 and had increased public **shareholding**. Other economic policies had begun to reduce inflation. The victory in the war against Argentina over the Falklands, despite much criticism of the war and how it was fought, had received favourable press coverage and was seen as leading a national revival.

The Labour party had split in 1981, with moderates breaking away from a party that had moved to the left with the election of Michael Foot as leader in 1980. The new Social Democratic party, together with their allies, the Liberals, polled 7.7 million votes, splitting the anti-Conservative vote. Previous Labour voters were turned away because of unpopular policies, such as nuclear disarmament and the nationalisation of industry. Foot's manifesto was called 'the longest suicide note in history'. Foot himself was not concerned enough with his image, and did not compare well on TV with the extremely forthright and confident Thatcher.

The election of 1987

The Conservatives increased their popular vote in this election, though actually lost 21 seats from their 1983 majority. Again, the SDP-Liberal alliance, which polled 7.3 million votes, split the left, and Labour had not, through either its leaders or its policies, been able to make the breakthrough.

Several Conservative policies were successful and popular:

- In key seats, the growth in shareholding and the ownership of council houses pleased aspiring middle-class voters.
- Inflation remained under control and was at its lowest level in the decade in 1986.
- Privatisation had increased and seemed, despite some teething problems, to be working.
- The burden of taxes had shifted from more unpopular direct taxes to indirect taxes.
- The deregulation of the financial sector had produced a financial boom engineered by the Chancellor of the Exchequer, Nigel Lawson.

Thatcher remained a charismatic if somewhat overbearing leader and her personal courage during an assassination attempt at Brighton had been admirable. She also had high standing internationally, fostering good relations with both the USA and with the USSR. Though there was no Falklands factor, Thatcher still kept the image of a strong and purposeful leader. The trade unions had been damaged by the unsuccessful **Miners' Strike** of 1984–85, during which the government had staunchly resisted the demands of striking workers. This contrasted with the much less successful attempts at union regulation under Wilson, Callaghan and Heath.

All three elections were not entirely the result of the success of Thatcher but did reflect the continuing appeal that her strongly articulated policies and decisive personality had among some voters.

Spectrum of importance

Below is a key question on why Thatcher won three elections and a list of possible points. Use your own knowledge and the information on the opposite page to reach a judgement about the relative importance of these points. Write the numbers on the spectrum below to indicate their relative importance. Having done this, write a brief justification of your placement, explaining why some of the factors are more important than others. The resulting diagram could be the basis of an essay plan.

Assess the reasons why Thatcher won three successive elections 1979 to 1987.

1 The weakness of the opposition

2 The popularity of the Falklands War

3 Her personal qualities and style

4 Social changes in Britain

5 Her policy towards the trade unions

6 The reduction of the rate of inflation

←──→

Least important   Most important

 Develop the detail

Below is a sample exam question and paragraph written in answer to this question. The paragraph contains a limited amount of detail. Annotate the paragraph to add additional detail to the answer.

'The weakness of Labour was the main reason for the length of Thatcher's tenure of office after 1979.' How far do you agree?

Thatcher was able to win three elections and remain in office for so long because Labour did not offer a convincing enough alternative. Its leaders did not appeal to the public as much as Thatcher and some of their policies seemed irrelevant and old fashioned. Labour was also quite divided over some issues. Some Labour manifestos were unpopular and one has been described as 'the longest suicide note in history' because changes in society had made it seem more like pre-war policies than applicable to the consumer society and the free market economy that Thatcher and her allies were promoting.

Economic policies, 1979–97

Thatcher's views on the economy

Thatcher identified four main economic problems:

1 Inflation. Prices had doubled in the 1970s.
2 Lack of investment, modernisation and economic stagnation.
3 Costly and unprofitable publicly owned industries and services.
4 A lack of incentive to modernise and increase productivity.

She strongly believed that her views were the only way to tackle these problems. Essentially, she thought that the state sector had been allowed to grow too much at the expense of private business and that state enterprises should be privatised and enterprise encouraged through the reduction of direct taxation. Government should not support 'lame duck' enterprises.

Thatcher saw dealing with inflation as a priority, and believed prices should be controlled by reducing the amount of money in circulation. According to Thatcher, regulation of wages and, therefore, incomes would not work; instead, the market must be allowed to determine prices and wages. Unemployment was preferable to continued inflation.

Thatcher's economic policies

- Privatisation began in October 1979 with the sale of British Petroleum and continued through the 1980s.
- Government no longer supported failing industries and these were allowed to stop production even though this resulted in unemployment.
- The Budgets of 1980 and 1981 aimed to reduce money in circulation by reducing government spending and raising indirect taxation.
- The Government's policies increased confidence abroad and the value of the pound rose.
- Direct taxes and taxes on businesses were reduced to free up money for investment.
- Interest rates remained high through the 1980s.
- The Financial Services Act of 1986 deregulated dealing in stocks and shares and opened up share trading.

The impact of Thatcher's economic policies

Price rise fell from 18% in 1980 to 4.5% in 1983 and there was a further fall in 1985–6. The stronger pound, changes in taxation and financial deregulation led to a growth in financial services while cuts and ending subsidies and rescues meant that weaker businesses failed. Unemployment rose sharply in the early 1980s: initially, 1.5 million was seen as high but the figure rose to 3 million by 1983 and did not begin to fall substantially until 1986. It was still over 2 million by 1990. Foreign investment increased; for example. the Japanese car firm Nissan established a plant in the North East. However, many new industries which emerged in the 1980s were not big employers and unemployment remained high.

Was there an economic revolution?

In many ways, there was an economic 'revolution'. There was a shift from the public sector to the private sector. Privatised industries remained in private hands, even after the end of Thatcher's period in office. There was more encouragement of enterprise, small businesses and investment on the stock market, as well as more home ownership and more individual shareholding. Industries were forced to become more competitive, and there were fewer restricted practices and lower labour costs.

Critics of Thatcher's policies pointed to a selfish, 'get rich quick' culture and less concern for the rights and conditions of workers. There was also a decline in manufacturing industry. Overall Britain lost 15 per cent of its manufacturing base and there was a greater divide between prosperous areas in London, the Midlands and the south-east and older industrial and mining areas. Government spending as a percentage of GDP did fall after 1984–85. However, this was not a permanent feature of economic life. Figures for 2010–11 were actually higher than in 1979. Thatcher's reductions in expenditure were not a new policy and the labour Chancellor of the Exchequer Denis Healy had made unpopular cuts in the 1970s.

After Thatcher, the economy offered more consumer choice; the balance between the state's role in the economy and that of the private sector did change, and the movement in employment from traditional industries towards services was accelerated.

Support or challenge?

Below is a sample essay question which asks you for a judgement on a statement. Using your knowledge and the information opposite decide whether these statements support or challenge the statement and tick the appropriate box.

'There was an economic revolution under Thatcher.' How far do you agree?

Statement	Support	Challenge
Home ownership increased.		
Some state-owned enterprises were privatised.		
Figures for government spending in 2011 were higher than they had been in 1979.		
The stock market was deregulated.		
More individuals owned shares than ever before.		
Monetarist policies were introduced.		
Subsidies and support for failing businesses were reduced.		
Interest rates remained high through the 1980s.		

Turning assertion into argument

Below are a sample exam question and a series of assertions. Read the question and then add a justification to each of the assertions to turn it into an argument.

How successful were Thatcher's economic policies after 1979?

Thatcher's policies fell heavily on the working class and this cannot be seen as a success.

_____

_____

Thatcher successfully encouraged more enterprise.

_____

_____

Thatcher successfully dealt with inflation.

_____

_____

Social policy

Thatcher thought that the professions should not be protected from change and should be brought more in line with good business practice. Greater control was imposed on education to try to ensure that Britain had a skilled workforce.

The NHS

A business model was applied to public health services.
- Hospitals became self-governing trusts and had to look after their own budgets.
- GPs were given a competitive choice in which NHS services to use.
- GPs were also responsible for managing their own budgets.

Education

As elsewhere, moves were made to make education more in line with business. State schools were allowed to opt out of local authority control and control their own budgets, and universities were expected to be more self funding and their budgets were cut.

In schools, a National Curriculum and a more rigorous inspection system were introduced in an attempt to ensure all pupils received a core of knowledge, and teaching standards were high. The distinction between O-levels, taken by supposedly more able students, and CSEs, taken by more vocational students, was ended with the introduction of GCSEs in 1986. In universities, there was also more quality control over teaching, and some lecturers lost their 'job for life'. Research was more controlled to ensure that universities were responsive to the needs of a modern society and economy.

Housing

In order to improve council tenants' sense of responsibility, there was a scheme to allow them to buy their own homes. This would reduce spending and also create more property owners who Thatcher thought would bring social stability to working-class areas.

Unrest

In terms of occupation and wealth, the balance shifted considerably in the 1980s away from traditional mining and industry towards finance, services, consumer goods, entertainment and manufacture and use of new technology. This meant winners and losers in society and new attitudes to the state and to wealth and its responsibilities.

Criticism came that employees enjoyed fewer rights; employers were more concerned with profits than welfare. Poverty was more apparent in the 1980s, with 'cardboard cities' and people sleeping rough. Urban centres in manufacturing areas became neglected and run down, while London and the south-east became visibly more prosperous. There was a constant undertow of criticism and this erupted into unrest on several occasions:
- There was rioting in Brixton, Liverpool and half a dozen other urban centres in the spring and summer of 1981.
- The Miners' Strike of 1984–85 saw outbreaks of violence and battles between strikers and police.
- In 1989, there was considerable unrest and demonstrations against the **Poll Tax**.

However, the level of political and social unrest was surprisingly low. The **Falklands War** of 1982 distracted opposition to domestic policies. The violence of the miners worried more moderate opponents. The government ensured that police forces were well paid and strong enough. Social discontent like the 1981 riots could not ally with political criticism, so the various discontents in Thatcher's Britain remained separate.

Delete as applicable

Below are a sample exam question and a paragraph written in answer to this question. Read the paragraph and decide which of the possible options (in bold) is most appropriate. Delete the least appropriate options and complete the paragraph by justifying your selection.

How far did Thatcher's policies bring about social change in Britain after 1979?

To a **great/fair/limited** extent the Thatcher governments brought about social change. The Britain of the 1990s was **very/somewhat/little** different from the Britain of 1979. A **key/quite important/not very important** element was the sale of council housing and the spread of share ownership. Economic change also had **a major/some/little** impact on society with the decline of the manufacturing industry and the growth in prosperity of the south and midlands. There was also a **very important/quite important/not very important** gap between the rich and poor. Changes in education had **a huge/some/little** impact, too.

Complete the paragraph · a

Below are a sample question and a paragraph written in answer to this question. The paragraph contains a point and examples, but lacks a concluding explanatory link back to the question. Complete the paragraph by adding this link. (Remember, 'assess' is not the same as 'explain'.)

Assess the consequences of social change under Margaret Thatcher 1979–90.

The 1980s saw a great deal of social change which had considerable consequences for Britain. An important development was the decline of manufacturing industry in some regions. The government no longer subsidised industries and allowed market forces to have their way. This resulted in urban decline and high unemployment in some areas while other regions, more dependent on goods and services did well, increasing the social divides in Britain. Another major consequence was the growth of the middle class as important changes encouraged home ownership and greater participation in shareholding. There was also social change in that there were new social attitudes towards business and social responsibility and the growth of a more 'get rich quick' culture.

_____

_____

Thatcher, her ministers and her fall

The impact of Thatcher's premiership

Thatcher faced some hostility from senior ministers not only because she was a woman but also because of her style and her political convictions. She had the support of some loyal ministers in the cabinet, especially William Whitelaw, her deputy, and Sir Keith Joseph. But there were others who resented her. Initially, she had to keep a balance between those who supported radical change and those who were more cautious – the so-called 'wets' like Michael Heseltine. However, with the support of backbench MPs and local constituencies, she gradually ousted the 'wets' and replaced them with people who supported her views.

Her style won her both admirers and enemies:
- Her energy and hard work ensured that she mastered the details of policies.
- She was intolerant of views and opinions which her rigid logic found to be flawed.
- She could be abrasive and tactless in discussion, but was also capable of great charm.

Increasing isolation

In 1982, Britain fought a short and successful war against Argentina, which had invaded the British Falklands islands. The Falklands War increased Thatcher's sense that she was shouldering great responsibility and while it gave her confidence, it also made her increasingly unwilling to listen to other views. After the independent-minded Michael Heseltine resigned in 1986, the cabinet was entirely dominated by those with her views. However, she felt the loss of her main adviser, William Whitelaw, who retired in 1987, and by 1989 she had fallen out with some key figures – her Chancellor, Nigel Lawson, and her Foreign Secretary, Geoffrey Howe. By 1990, the forcefulness for which she was so admired had become too overbearing for her colleagues and for her popularity across the country.

The fall of Thatcher

By 1990, Thatcher was beset with problems, which eventually led to her fall. Firstly, the economic progress of the mid-1980s was faltering. Inflation was rising again and the Government had relied on high interest rates to control the boom which it had created. Secondly, the Tories were obviously divided about the issue of Europe and this made them vulnerable to an electoral defeat. Thatcher had serious disagreements with her colleagues Lawson and Howe over Europe. They had wanted to join the European **Exchange Rate Mechanism (ERM)** but she refused, instinctively distrusting any closer links with the EEC. In the end Thatcher agreed to join the ERM, which made her seem weaker.

Thirdly, there were signs of a change in the public mood:
- The Tories did badly in the European elections in 1989.
- They lost in by-elections in 1989 and 1990.
- Public opinion polls put Labour ahead.

This all led to Tory rebels putting forward a little-known candidate, Sir Anthony Meyer, to stand against Thatcher in a leadership election and he won 33 votes.

Finally, the policy of the Poll Tax was very unpopular. This 'Community Charge' introduced in 1988 changed local government finance by taxing individuals, not property. It led to protests and a violent riot in London in March 1990.

The key elements in Thatcher's fall

There was a real fear among Conservatives that they would lose the next election. As her unpopularity grew, many colleagues remembered the signs of contempt and rudeness which they had accepted when Thatcher seemed to be successful and popular. The immediate trigger for her downfall was when Thatcher's senior cabinet minister Howe made a devastating speech against her on 13 November 1990. This prompted her old enemy Michael Heseltine to stand against her for the leadership and, while he failed, he won enough votes for there to have to be another vote. She asked her ministers' opinion and there was a consensus that she should resign. As a result, Thatcher resigned on 22 November 1990.

Simple essay style

Below is a sample exam question. Use your own knowledge and information on the opposite page to produce a plan for this question. Choose four general points, and provide three pieces of specific information to support each general point. The introduction should list the points to be discussed in the essay. The conclusion should summarise the key points and justify which was the most important.

'Poor relations with her ministers was the most important reason for the fall of Margaret Thatcher.' How far do you agree?

 Introducing an argument a

Below are a sample exam question, a list of points to be made in the essay, and a simple introduction and conclusion for the essay. Read the question, the key points, and the introduction and conclusion. Rewrite the introduction and conclusion in order to develop an argument that deals directly with 'assess'.

Assess the reasons for the fall of Thatcher.

Key points:

- Her style of management
- The Poll tax
- Tory divisions about Europe
- Resentment about the Westland Affair
- By election results and public opinion

Introduction

There were many reasons for the fall of Thatcher, some of them were long term and some were more related to the situation in 1990. The widespread popularity which she had achieved in the Falklands War had declined and she was finding it more difficult to achieve unity in her party.

Conclusion

Thatcher had alienated many in her government and her party by her abrasive style of management, and this was important when it came to her fall. There was also less economic success than previously and some felt that she was taking a short-sighted view of Britain's future in Europe.

Major's Government, 1990–97

After Thatcher resigned on 22 November 1990, her Foreign Secretary, John Major, announced his decision to stand in the Conservative leadership election. He won the contest on 27 November and became Prime Minister the following day.

What problems did John Major face?

- He had risen quickly and did not have a strong body of support or a record of success.
- The Conservatives continued to be divided about Europe.
- Labour was encouraged and revitalised by Thatcher's fall and the divisions within the Tories.
- Europe moved towards greater economic and political integration with the Maastricht Treaty of 1991, which left Major having to negotiate opting out of the single currency and the Social Chapter, but also facing intense criticism from the Eurosceptics in his own party.
- There was an economic downturn as the Government was forced to take measures to stop inflation.

Why did Major win the election of 1992?

To the surprise of many, the Conservatives won the 1992 General Election. This was largely due to Major himself, who had campaigned very effectively. There had been an obvious change in the style of government, with Major being a less divisive and abrasive figure than Thatcher. Major's quieter style contrasted with the more flamboyant personality of the Labour leader, Neil Kinnock. Also, relying on opinion polls, Kinnock was over-confident, and gave the impression that he assumed victory was his.

Why did Major lose the election of 1997?

Though Major had increased his popular vote in 1992, he lost 21 seats. In 1997, however, he faced a very large defeat. Labour won its biggest majority since 1945, with 418 seats as opposed to the Tories' 165. The reasons for this were a combination of Conservative problems and a turnaround for Labour.

In 1992, there had been a damaging episode when Britain had been forced to withdraw from the European Exchange Rate Mechanism after the pound fell sharply in value. Major and his Chancellor, Norman Lamont, attempted to prevent this by raising interest rates to new highs before the attempt failed and Britain had to withdraw. The divisions within the Conservative Party over Europe generally got worse and feelings in the party ran high.

In contrast, Labour was revitalised after Kinnock resigned following Labour's fourth consecutive defeat in the 1992 election. First, the short period of leadership of John Smith produced a moderate and well-respected leader who became popular. Smith died in 1994, and Tony Blair was elected, another popular and articulate figure. By 1997, 'New Labour' had emerged as a unifying and attractive party.

What were the elements of 'New Labour'?

- A relative young and dynamic leader who communicated well.
- The party accepted some key elements of the Thatcher years and did not threaten those people who had gained, for example the financial sector and owners of shares and council houses.
- Blair broke with the past by finally abandoning nationalisation of industry – Clause IV of the 1918 constitution.
- Labour's press and public relations was handled with great professional skill and it got the support of some key media elements like the Sun newspaper.
- Labour was obviously less divided than the Conservatives.
- Labour offered popular policies and effective 'sound bites' like 'Education, education, education' and 'Tough on crime, tough on the causes of crime'.

After such a long period of Conservative rule, with the new millennium approaching and with less than dynamic Conservative leadership and economic performance, many felt that it was time for a change.

Identify an argument

Below are a series of definitions, a sample exam question and two sample conclusions. One of the conclusions achieves a high level because it contains an argument. The other achieves a lower level because it contains only description and assertion. Identify which is which. The mark scheme on page 7 will help you.

- Description: a detailed account.
- Assertion: a statement of fact or an opinion, which is not supported by a reason.
- Reason: a statement that explains or justifies something.
- Argument: an assertion justified with a reason.

How successful was John Major as Prime Minister?

Sample 1

John Major became Prime Minister after the fall of Thatcher. His rise was a surprise because he had not had wide experience of government and was not from the traditional Tory background. He changed the style of government and he did not share Thatcher's anti-European views. He took measures to deal with economic problems and he signed the Maastricht treaty in 1991 that brought Britain more into line with Europe. He was successful in the 1992 election but then encountered problems with the ERM and with increasing hostility within his party. He did not win the 1997 election in the face of an effective campaign run by Tony Blair and New Labour.

Sample 2

John Major took over as Prime Minister at a difficult time when the party was split over Europe and when the country was showing its impatience with Thatcher's personality and policies. Yet Major managed to increase the popular vote in the election of 1992, something that shows a high level of political success. He offered a distinct change of style and policy from Thatcher and successfully exploited the need for a change while taking advantage of Labour's weaknesses. However, there was less success after 1992 because of economic difficulties and because New Labour offered a more dynamic political challenge which Major, because of both his personality and because of ever-widening rifts with his party, found it difficult to deal with.

Develop the detail

Below are a sample exam answer and a paragraph written in answer to this question. The paragraph contains limited amount of detail. Annotate the paragraph to add additional detail to the answer.

How far do problems over Europe account for the failure of John Major to be re-elected in 1997?

Though Major faced a powerful opponent in New Labour, with its dynamic and effective leader, the fundamental problems that Major faced and which made him less electable were over Europe. The Conservatives were so obviously divided that it became hard for many to think that Major could carry on governing. It seemed that the Eurosceptics were reactionary and were also associated with backward-looking domestic views. Blair seemed, in comparison, to be leading a united and more modern party.

Exam focus

Below is a sample exam question and model answer. Read the essay and the comments around it.

How successful were Thatcher's economic policies, 1979–90?

Thatcher saw Britain as suffering from long term decline in 1979 with inflation running high and with industry suffering from lack of investment and high costs, making Britain uncompetitive. Her solutions were based on the reduction of government interference in the economy and freeing enterprise, and control of inflation by monetary policy. She was more successful in some areas than others and the effects of policies aimed at growth meant greater income and regional inequality, but there were areas of economic success, particularly in the control of inflation.

> This sets up the key elements in the policies and offers a balanced view. The judgement could be sharper, however.

The centrepiece of her economic policy was to deal with inflation. She saw this as making Britain uncompetitive, hurting exports and leading to a cycle of high wage claims. The rate at which prices rose fell from 18 per cent in 1980 to 4.5 per cent in 1983. The reduction in government borrowing and the increased indirect taxes took money out of the economy, as did high interest rates. There was a particularly sharp drop in inflation from 1981 to 1983, then again from 1985 to 1986. Though prices rose from late 1987, at no time did the inflation rate reach the high levels of the 1970s. Controlling inflation increased confidence and boosted investment. It was particularly good for Britain's financial sector. However, critics argued that the costs were high in terms of rising unemployment, and also that Thatcher was not doing anything new and that Denis Healy had also followed deflationary measures in the late 1970s. It was also argued that cuts in spending and failure to help ailing industries put financial stability before supporting Britain's industrial and manufacturing base.

> This offers a balanced treatment of this element and deals directly with the question of 'how successful'. It is better to keep the pros and cons of the inflation policy together in one section.

In terms of manufacturing, the privatisation of key infrastructure and the failure to support industries resulted in Britain losing 15 per cent of its manufacturing base. Thatcher argued that market forces resulted in more competitive, leaner and fitter industries; and that tax cuts and reform of union law helped to encourage investment and reduced costs. However, critics pointed to an increasing amount of money having to go on unemployment benefits and to the loss of valuable skills and industrial capital as firms went out of business. There was also concern about the social effects on communities like the coal villages when staple industries were allowed to decline.

> There could be more detail here but the section is again balanced and is consistent with the argument in the opening.

The strengthening of the services and the financial sector and the encouragement of high-tech industries did bring about an economic transformation. Deregulation of the City encouraged a boom. The selling of shares in nationalised industries spread shareholding and boosted capitalism, but there were social costs and growing inequality between north and south.

> The answer follows the balanced analysis of the opening.

Britain's economic reputation grew under Thatcher. The City enjoyed great prestige. British entrepreneurs were admired. Britain no longer suffered from heavy losses through strikes. Investment came into the country, for example when Nissan established a plant in the north-east. Thatcher's model was admired by conservative economists and governments around the world. However, some of the relative change in Britain's status was more to do with economic decline in the growth rate of other European countries. The new growth areas were not big employers so unemployment continued to be high and to absorb a high level of GNP, including the revenues derived from North Sea Oil.

In the end, the consequences of economic change were too mixed to argue that Thatcher's policies were really successful. One objective, the lowering of inflation, was pursued at the expense of other desirable aims and caused too many problems. The privatisation and the sale of council houses had mixed results. The loss of social housing meant that more had to be spent on welfare, as did heavy regional unemployment. The dependence on financial services, high levels of consumer spending and oil revenues was in the end dangerous. Trade surpluses fell away after 1984. Cuts in taxation did not always lead to the hoped-for investment and social instability was a high price to pay for some of the successes.

The conclusion does follow the arguments and is neatly expressed and analytical – the answer does rather come down more on the side of not very successful than the opening suggests.

This is a very strong answer which offers a balanced view and whose overall judgement follows on from the analysis presented. The opening sets out a clear analysis which is pursued in the essay and is generally relevant.

Exam focus activity

Using the comments and the mark scheme on page 7, make a list of additional features, both in terms of supporting detail but also argument, that would enable this answer to reach the highest level. Remember that even an answer that is awarded full marks is not a perfect answer, but one that best fits with the level descriptors in the mark scheme.

7 Britain's position in the world, 1951–97

Relations with the USA and the USSR

Relations with the USA

After the Second World War, fears of Soviet expansion contributed to the onset of the Cold War. Relations between Britain and the USA consequently became closer.

- The USA gave Britain financial aid under the **Marshall Aid** scheme.
- Britain and the US cooperated over the **Berlin Blockade**, 1948–49.
- Britain and the USA were members of the North Atlantic Treaty Organization (NATO), which was established in 1949.
- There was talk of a 'special relationship'.
- In 1950–51, Britain and the USA sent troops to defend South Korea against an invasion by the Chinese-backed Communist North Korea.
- Britain joined the US in the Geneva agreement which divided Vietnam in 1954.

However, there were strains and Britain was not an equal partner as its economic problems and decline as a world power limited its possible military assistance. Two conflicts also strained relations. Britain's intervention in Suez in 1956 (see page 92) was not supported by the USA and then when the USA became involved in a war in Vietnam, Britain did not offer military support because of Britain's economic problems and the lack of public support for the US, and tried to bring about a peace settlement. In the Cuban Missile Crisis of 1962 which, perhaps, was the closest the world came to a hot, rather than a cold war, the USA did not act in close co-operation with Britain.

Thatcher and Reagan

Thatcher and Reagan were both staunch opponents of Communism. They undertook well-publicised visits to one another and they established strong personal ties. They agreed on many policy issues such as opposing UN sanctions against South Africa and helped each other militarily: Reagan lent some US assistance to the British in the Falklands War and Thatcher allowed the USA to use British air bases. However, there were areas of disagreement:

- Thatcher was sceptical about Reagan's **'Star Wars'** initiative.
- She was worried that Reagan might make too many concessions on nuclear disarmament.

- She disliked the US invasion of Grenada to remove a left-wing government in 1983.

Cooperation after 1990

The UK and USA maintained strong ties after the Thatcher–Reagan years. They co-operated in the First Gulf War in 1993 to remove Iraq's troops from Kuwait after an invasion by Saddam Hussein, and the two countries collaborated in UN efforts to stop violence in the former Yugoslavia in 1995.

Relations with the USSR

In many ways, mutual suspicion, distrust and disapproval characterised Britain's relationship with the USSR. Britain's defence planning envisaged the USSR as the major threat for the Cold War period and Britain and the USA kept a military presence in Germany to guard against Soviet expansion. Both the UK and USA agreed to the rearming of West Germany and its inclusion in NATO, which the USSR opposed, and both countries opposed North Korean expansion in 1950, which had the backing of the USSR.

Russia disapproved of the Suez Crisis and was critical of Britain's imperialism generally while Britain was critical of the USSR's repression of unrest in eastern Europe, especially in the Hungarian Revolt of 1956 and the Czech crisis of 1968. Britain condemned the building of the Berlin Wall in 1961 and the Soviet invasion of Afghanistan in 1980. Both sides accused the other of espionage, and a low point in relations over this was the expulsion of over a hundred Soviet diplomats from Britain in 1971.

However, there were frequent attempts to relieve tensions. After the fall of Stalin in 1953 there was greater contact between the two sides and more state visits. For example, Khrushchev visited Britain in 1956 and Macmillan went to Moscow in 1959. Despite her strong criticisms of Communism, under Thatcher Britain established good relations with Gorbachev, and there were state visits in 1984. The fall of the USSR's control in eastern Europe in 1989 and the reforms which brought about the end of Communism and the break up of the USSR in 1991 were welcomed in Britain, and brought about a new phase of Anglo–Russian relations.

Turning an assertion into argument

Below are a sample exam question and a series of assertions. Read the exam question and then add a justification to each of the assertions to turn it into an argument

How well did Britain manage its relationship with the USA from 1951 to 1997?

British relations with the USA were poorly managed at the time of the Suez Crisis because

_____

_____

The strongest relationship between the USA and Britain was during the Thatcher years because

_____

_____

It was clear that Britain and the US were not equal partners for much of the 1950s and 1960s because

_____

_____

Develop the detail

Below are a sample exam question and a paragraph written in answer to the question. The paragraph contains a limited amount of detail. Annotate the paragraph to add additional detail to the answer.

Assess the reasons for Britain's changing relations with the USSR.

Britain had hoped that relations with the USSR would improve, but the USSR disliked Britain's policy in West Germany. Britain for its part disliked the policy of the USSR in eastern Europe. Personal contacts were important, though, in improving relations, as were changes in the USSR.

Britain and the United Nations

British support for the UN

Britain had a historic role in the founding and the early development of the United Nations and the first meetings of the general assembly and the Security Council were in London in January 1946. Since then, Britain has been an active and supportive member of the UN.

- Britain has always been a permanent member of the Security Council.
- Britain has been a major contributor to the UN budget and in 2013–15 was still providing 6.7 per cent of the total.
- British-born officials have played a significant role in the agencies of the UN.
- Britain has had one judge on the International Court of Justice at the Hague.
- Britain has been a member of the important Economic and Social Council.
- British governments have been anxious to obtain UN support for policies, which has boosted the authority of the UN. The war against Iraq in 1991 was justified by UN condemnation of Iraq's invasion of Kuwait.

British forces have taken part in peacekeeping missions and in UN military actions. The most prolonged conflict was the Korean War of 1950–53 in which British forces took part in a war to prevent North Korea, backed by China and the USSR, from taking over independent South Korea. The other major contribution was the deployment of British forces in the former Yugoslavia from 1992 to 1995 to prevent ethnic cleansing by Serbian troops in Bosnia and Croatia. British participation in other peacekeeping activities has been less developed but British troops have been part of the peacekeeping force in Cyprus since 1964.

British conflict with the UN

Despite the close ties with the UN listed above, Britain has also asserted its own interests and those of its allies. Britain has had a right of veto, which it has used 32 times since 1956, such as when it vetoed resolutions over demands for majority rule in Rhodesia between 1963 and 1976 as Britain did not wish to take military action.

One major example of Britain acting outside the UN is the Suez Crisis. In 1956, Britain, France and Israel allied to attack Egypt after Nasser had nationalised the Suez Canal. The UN was not consulted, though Britain accepted the intervention of UN peacekeeping forces when it was clear that domestic and international opinion was against the intervention. Here are some other examples of Britain going against the UN:

- When the UN wished to condemn US bombing of Libya in 1986, Thatcher joined the USA in vetoing the critical resolution.
- Britain did little to limit conflicts in the Congo and Rwanda.
- Britain resented and largely ignored criticism within the UN about its colonial policies.

British military support for the UN has been relatively limited. Only 2,500 troops were deployed to support humanitarian aid and peacekeeping in the former Yugoslavia. British membership of NATO has been more significant in terms of its foreign and defence policy.

Support or challenge

Below is a sample exam question which asks how far you agree with a specific statement. Below this are a series of general statements which are relevant to the question. Using your own knowledge and the information on the opposite page decide whether these statements challenge the statement in the question and tick the appropriate box.

'Membership of the UN was very important to Britain between 1951 and 1997 in maintaining its status as a great power.' How far do you agree?

Statement	Support	Challenge
2,500 troops were supplied to support peacekeeping in the former Yugoslavia.		
Britain used her veto over 25 times in this period.		
Britain provided over 6% of the UN's budget.		
Britain is a permanent member of the Security Council.		
Britain took a leading part in supporting the UN in the Korean War.		
Britain did not consult the UN before sending troops to the Suez Canal Zone in 1956.		

 Delete as applicable

Below are a sample exam question and a paragraph written in answer to the question. Read the paragraph and decide which of the possible options (in bold) is most appropriate. Delete the least appropriate options and complete the paragraph by justifying your selection.

How great a role did Britain play in the United Nations between 1951 and 1997?

British support for and participation in the UN has been **very consistent/not always consistent/completely inconsistent.** Britain has **always/sometimes/rarely** supported its peacekeeping activities. Britain has **always/sometimes/rarely** responded to criticism of its colonial role. British national interests and its need to support its allies, such as the USA, have **never/sometimes/always** influenced its policy to the UN and its use of its veto. The early importance of Britain in the establishment of the UN has been **important/unimportant** in shaping British attitudes to the UN.

Britain's role in Europe

Britain's relationship with Europe has been controversial since the Second World War.

Britain as an outsider in the move to European unity

During the 1950s, there was considerable scepticism about joining a united Europe at a time when Britain also had strong links with the Commonwealth and a special relationship with the USA. Britain, therefore, remained outside the European Coal and Steel Community in 1952 and did not take part in the discussions which led to the Treaty of Rome in 1955 which established the European Economic Community. It was not until 1961 that Britain applied to join the EEC but its application was rejected. This was because France vetoed Britain's membership, largely because its President, Charles de Gaulle, doubted British commitment to a more united Europe. Britain eventually applied to join the EEC in 1972, and offcially joined in 1973 under Heath's Conservative Government. However, debates about Britain's membership did not disappear and when Wilson became Labour Prime Minister, he decided to hold a referendum in 1975 to decide the issue. The 'remain' side won but a third of voters were against membership.

In the 1980s, there were disagreements under Thatcher about the EEC budget contributions, and Thatcher made it clear that she opposed the European vision of a more united Europe. Though Britain was briefly a member of the ERM and signed the Maastricht Treaty in 1991 that was committed to greater economic and political union, it did not accept the idea of a common currency and has never joined the euro. Throughout the 1990s, Euroscepticism was strong in the Conservative party.

Britain as a major player in Europe

Despite not joining the EEC until fairly late, Britain still played a major role in Europe up until it became a member. For example:

- Britain was a major power in the North Atlantic Treaty Organization set up in 1949.
- Britain had taken the initiative in establishing the European Free Trade Area (EFTA) in 1960.

European Free Trade Area

Seven European countries which were not in the EEC created the European Free Trade Area in 1960 which was a looser structure than the EEC. Its members (the UK, Denmark, Norway, Sweden, Austria, Switzerland and Portugal) abolished trade tariffs but were free to set their own tariffs with non-member countries, allowing Britain to maintain strong trading links with the Commonwealth.

Britain persisted with its attempts to join the EEC after de Gaulle's retirement in 1969. Heath was an avid European and Britain finally joined the Common Market when he was Prime Minister. As a member of the EEC, which became the European Union in 1993, British statesmen served as European commissioners and Britain:

- accepted the bulk of European regulations and was a contributor to European institutions
- accepted unpopular policies such as restricting Commonwealth cheap food imports and being part of the Common Agricultural Policy
- accepted restrictions on sovereignty, and elections to a European Parliament based on a system of proportional representation not used in British parliamentary elections.

It is also worth noting during the period 1951–97, there was no organised and influential anti-European party in Britain.

! Complete the paragraph

Below are a sample exam question and a paragraph written in answer to this question. The paragraph contains a point and specific examples, but lacks a concluding explanatory link back to the question. Complete the paragraph adding this link in the space provided.

How great a role did Britain play in Europe between 1951 and 1997?

After a long period in which Britain did not play a major role in a united Europe, it applied to join the European Economic Community in 1961, but its membership was rejected because of French opposition. When Britain joined in 1973, it played a significant part in Europe, but as Europe moved to closer union, Britain became more reluctant to accept the ideals of those who wished for currency union. The experience of joining and then having to leave the ERM and the political unpopularity of losing the pound sterling made Britain sceptical about a common currency.

_____

_____

♦ Eliminate irrelevance   a

Below are a sample exam question and a paragraph written in answer to the question. Read the paragraph and identify parts of the paragraph that are not directly relevant to the question. Draw a line through the information that is irrelevant and justify your deletions in the margin.

Assess the reasons for opposition to British participation in a united Europe between 1951 and 1997.

Britain had experienced considerable problems in foreign policy in the 1950s such as the Suez Crisis and had also lost much of its Empire. This meant that statesmen looked more towards greater union with Europe, especially as growth rates in the EEC were higher than in Britain and Britain needed outlets in Europe for its trade. However, before Britain's application in 1961 there were many who were sceptical about Europe because of the economic advantages of cheap food from the commonwealth and a belief that Britain was closely linked both to its former empire and to the USA. It was not until 1972 that Britain successfully applied to join Europe as de Gaulle had vetoed our entry.

British nuclear policy

After the USA's development of the atomic bomb and its use on Japan in May 1945, there was a danger that the US monopoly would give it domination over Europe. Both the USSR and Britain decided to build atomic weapons. Britain's decision came in 1947 because it was worried that in the event of an attack from the USSR the USA might decide not to support Europe. An invasion of Germany would involve Britain in another war and it lacked enough conventional forces to meet the Soviet threat. Britain also still saw itself as a great power and having an independent deterrent seemed essential.

Why did this become controversial?

Over time, the devastating effects of the bombing of Hiroshima and Nagasaki became better known and there was increasing fear that nuclear war would bring 'mutually assured destruction' after the Soviet Union developed their own atomic weapons. Some scientists had become uneasy about the power of the weapons they had created and there was a substantial body of opinion within Britain who opposed nuclear weapons on ethical grounds. The Campaign for Nuclear disarmament, led by Canon Collins, began in 1958 and achieved a lot of publicity due to its easily recognisable emblem and the marches it held from the nuclear weapons research establishment at Aldermarston to London. In 1960, as many as 100,000 marchers took part. Many in the Labour movement shared the concern but there were deep divisions. The Labour left winger Aneurin Bevan made the point that Britain would have little negotiating power in world affairs without an independent deterrent. It was believed that the only defence against Soviet aggression was the threat of nuclear war and that the West needed a nuclear arsenal alongside smaller conventional forces.

Public unease about the dangers of nuclear war destroying the world and the costs involved led to some agreements about non-proliferation in 1963 and 1968, but developments in the 1970s in missile technology led to the deployment of intercontinental missiles by both NATO and the USSR which were capable of destroying targets anywhere in Europe within minutes. This led to more domestic protest in Britain with the setting up of a women-only protest camp at the US air base at Greenham Common which lasted for 19 years.

As the Cold War remained 'cold' despite some major crises, especially in 1962 with the Cuban Missile Crisis, the argument of the danger they posed was countered with the view that nuclear weapons had been uniquely successful in keeping peace. The collapse of the Soviet Union did not, however, result in the scrapping of nuclear missiles. Britain has maintained that its missiles, carried on submarines, were its most important line of defence. This claim has been challenged as the Cold War has given way to regional conflicts and the threat from terrorism which cannot be met by nuclear strikes.

Developments since 1947 – an 'independent' deterrent?

The British independent deterrent became less independent after 1962 when the USA supplied Britain with Polaris missiles and also when Britain allowed the USA to use air bases for a possible nuclear strike. Britain did take part in its own right in banning nuclear testing in space and under water in 1963 and in reducing the proliferation of weapons in 1968, but it was not part of the important Strategic Arms Limitations Talks Agreements in 1972 and 1979 between the USA and the USSR. In 1987, Thatcher persuaded Reagan to supply Britain with the Trident missiles carried by Britain's nuclear submarines. By 1991, Britain had fewer than 200 weapons all assigned to the four Trident submarines, which came into service 1994–98.

Identify an argument

Below are a series of definitions, a sample exam question and two sample conclusions. One of the conclusions achieves a high level because it contains an argument. The other achieves a lower level because it contains only description and assertion. Identify which is which. The mark scheme on page 7 will help you.

- Description: a detailed account.
- Assertion: a statement of fact or an opinion, which is not supported by a reason.
- Reason: a statement that explains or justifies something.
- Argument: an assertion justified with a reason.

Assess the reasons why British nuclear defence policy was so controversial 1945–97?

Sample 1

The decision was taken in 1947 to build an independent British atomic bomb because of the danger the Government felt the country was in from the Soviet Union. Some thought that this was exaggerated and some felt that the Soviet Union should actually have its own atomic weapons to feel on equal terms with the West. It became more controversial when the size and destructive capacity of weapons grew with the development of hydrogen bombs and when it became clear how much destruction had been caused. Many people felt that it was immoral for Britain to have weapons which could destroy the world, but others thought that it was the only way to keep the peace. Some thought that when there were agreements about test bans and proliferation that nuclear weapons could be controlled, but others were more worried by the crises that kept arising, for example over Berlin and Cuba, and the danger that these might escalate in mutually assured destruction despite the crises. There was also controversy about the dependence that Britain had on the USA for nuclear missiles after Polaris in 1992. More controversy was caused by the Greenham Common protests as it was felt that more lay behind it than just the nuclear issue as it was an all-woman protest against a male weapons policy. By the 1990s, the reduction of weapons and the reliance on nuclear submarines caused controversy because it was felt that Britain's security problems were no longer from the USSR and this option had become dangerous and irrelevant, while others felt that the submarines gave Britain potential power worldwide in case it was threatened.

Sample 2

The most significant controversies arose from the moral issues behind Britain's nuclear defence policies. Though there was argument about cost and also about whether after 1991 there was any point in maintaining a nuclear policy after the end of the Cold War, the main elements were in terms of the morality of the nuclear option. This lay behind the campaign for nuclear disarmament led by a clergymen Canon Collins and supported by those who were horrified at the damage done to Japan by nuclear bombs and the unacceptability of taking a decision which might end the world. The passionate and prolonged protest at Greenham Common was on the basis of women's feelings about the need for peace rather than strategic or economic arguments, even though a woman, Margaret Thatcher was an equally passionate supporter of nuclear weapons as a means of keeping peace. Arguments within the Labour Party were again on moral grounds and whether a progressive social democratic party should support weapons of such destruction. There were other arguments particularly associated with the political aspects of the domination of the USA over British nuclear policy and also of the irrelevance in terms of defence strategy of relying on four nuclear submarines in a world which was threatened not by two great nuclear power blocs but by dangerous local conflicts and global terrorism and instability. However, for most of the period, the major controversy – as evidenced by the mass marches of the 1960s – was about the humanitarian aspects.

Britain's response to crises, 1951–97

REVISED

The Korean War, 1950–53

Britain joined a UN force to defend South Korea 1950–53 against invasion by Communist North Korea. There were several reasons why Britain participated. Firstly, in the Cold War atmosphere Britain was committed to resisting Communist aggression and preventing Communist expansion. In this particular case, Britain was also worried as it still had possessions in Asia. Secondly, Britain still thought of itself as an important world power. Britain was a major founding force in the UN and felt it had to be supported to remain credible. Finally, it was vital for Britain's security to maintain links with the USA and support its stand against aggression.

Results

As a result of the war, NATO was strengthened due to the fear of further Communist aggression. Britain had confirmed its 'special relationship' with the USA, although this was as a junior partner as the British contribution was far less than that of the USA. However, the war was costly as 700 British and Commonwealth troops had been killed and Britain's economic problems were made worse by the high defence expenditure involved.

The Suez Crisis, 1956

Britain allied with France and Israel to attack Egypt, whose nationalist ruler, Nasser, had nationalised the Suez Canal. There were several reasons:

- The Suez Canal was a vital route way – two-thirds of oil supplies to Europe passed through it.
- The UK feared the potential spread of USSR-backed Arab nationalism.
- Eden saw Nasser as a dictator who must be opposed.
- Eden assumed that the USA would approve and that Nasser could easily be overthrown.

Results

The invasion failed, and Nasser's position was actually strengthened as a result. Britain's actions brought much international criticism. The USA felt that it hadn't been consulted and opposed the whole plan, while the USSR criticised British imperialism and strengthened ties with Nasser. The Suez Crisis also distracted the West, allowing the USSR to brutally crush the Hungarian Revolt that same year. For Britain, it demonstrated that it was no longer a great imperial power who could act on its own at will. It directly led to the resignation of Eden in 1957.

The Falklands Crisis, 1982

Britain sent a force to retake the Falklands islands, which had been occupied by Argentina. This was a risk as there was no guarantee of international support and British forces would have to fight a large Argentinian force thousands of miles from home and the task force was vulnerable to air attack. The decision to retake the island was made because British prestige as a major power was at stake and importantly, the military advised the Government that Britain could succeed. Thatcher's reputation as a strong leader demanded decisive action and military action demonstrated to the USSR that aggression would not succeed. Crucially, Thatcher also gained support for military action from:

- both the UN and the EU
- most of the British press
- all political parties
- the USA which gave intelligence support and the use of the US base on Ascension.

Results

The reputation of British forces rose as they succeeded in retaking the Falklands, and Thatcher's popularity at home increased, despite the high financial cost of the war itself and subsequent garrisoning of the islands. As a consequence of its defeat, the Argentine military regime fell, but there was continuing resentment in Argentina towards Britain, even though no further action was taken.

The Gulf War, 1991

Britain sent forces as part of US-led coalition to liberate Kuwait after an Iraqi invasion in order to:

- show solidarity with the USA, its vital Arab allies in the Gulf and the UN. Britain provided the third largest contingent of troops in the US-led coalition.
- prevent further invasions from Saddam Hussein, the Iraq leader
- protect oil supplies
- support international law and order
- show that Britain was still a major power and that John Major was not weaker than Thatcher had been in 1982 – even though Kuwait was not a British colony.

Results

Coalition forces succeeded in liberating Kuwait and British air power played a key role. This fostered an ongoing commitment to maintaining peace in the region. British relations with the USA were strengthened, but action in Kuwait indirectly led to further war in Iraq in 2003, which had far greater consequences.

Mind map

Use the information on the opposite page to add detail to the mind map below.

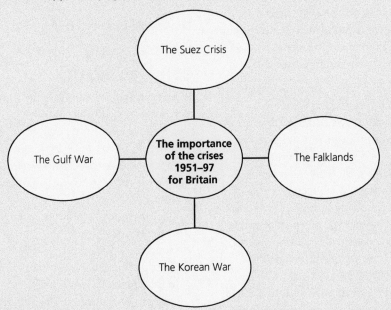

The Suez Crisis

The Gulf War

The importance of the crises 1951–97 for Britain

The Falklands

The Korean War

 ## You're the examiner

Below are a sample exam question and a paragraph written in answer to the question. Read the paragraph and the mark scheme provided on page 7. Decide which level you would award the paragraph. Write the level below, along with a justification for your decision.

'The Falklands War was the most serious crisis which Britain faced between 1951 and 1997.' How far do you agree?

> The Falklands was a major crisis for Britain. It blew up suddenly before Britain was prepared and it was by no means certain that Britain would be able to solve the crisis by military action. It affected British territory directly and the Falkland islanders could legitimately look to Britain for protection. To back down would have been to admit that Britain was not a great power, but to take action risked heavy loss of life for the task force. There was no guarantee of international support since the Falklands were part of the British Empire and many countries were suspicious of imperialism. The logistics of sending a task force to fight thousands of miles from home and being subject to possible air attacks were risky. A small British force had to face the possibility of a very large Argentine army. If they had been defeated, then the political consequences for Thatcher would have been considerable. Other crises were also serious, but this was the most serious.

Level:

_____

Reason for choosing that level:

_____

_____

Britain's policy towards decolonisation and the Commonwealth, 1951–97

There was no intention to decolonise during and immediately after the Second World War, but during the period 1951–97 Britain granted independence to most of its colonies. This was due to several interlinked reasons.

The Second World War had shown Britain's weakness to its subject people and lowered British prestige as Japan had conquered Britain's south-east Asian colonies easily. This encouraged nationalist movements in British colonies demanding independence, and there was a marked growth in support for these movements, especially after India was granted independence in 1947. There were also hopes of post-independence stability and continuing links to Britain with the prospect of strong nationalist leaders who also seemed to make resistance to independence difficult. For example, Nkrumah in Ghana was an effective leader, but offered to keep an independent Ghana in the Commonwealth. In the end, the colonies were not seen as any more beneficial to Britain under direct rule than the same countries would be as members of the Commonwealth.

International opinion towards empire was hostile. The USA disapproved and the USSR and its allies denounced British Imperialism. In 1955, many newly independent nations denounced colonial rule and established the **Non-Alignment movement**. Also, the greater influence of countries outside Europe in the United Nations led to condemnation of imperialism and made it difficult for Britain to conduct international relations as an Imperial power.

There were also economic reasons. Britain's economic problems made it hard for it to sustain control over colonies and also to invest in them. The costs of defending British rule were too high and bloody colonial wars, such as that in Kenya against the Mau Mau rebels or in Cyprus against EOKA opposition, were unpopular at home and made Britain reluctant to use military force, for example, against Rhodesia.

Finally, British political leaders accepted the need to decolonise. In 1960, Macmillan made the famous 'Wind of Change' speech in Africa and from the 1970s Britain was moving away from its economic links to its former empire and more towards Europe.

How well did Britain make the transition from Empire to Commonwealth?

In many ways, Britain made the transition from Empire to Commonwealth successfully:

- The decision of the newly independent states of India, Pakistan and Ceylon (modern-day Sri Lanka) to stay within the Commonwealth was a success as it set a precedent for other colonies to maintain links with Britain.
- The Commonwealth supported Britain's involvement in the Korean War.
- Commonwealth meetings and declarations of principles maintained Britain's influence, and loyalty to the Queen has been a significant element in keeping cultural, economic and diplomatic ties.
- The decision of South Africa to rejoin the Commonwealth after the end of **Apartheid** in 1994 was an indication of its success.

On the other hand:

- The colonial wars in Kenya (1952–63), Cyprus (1955–60) and Malaya (1948–60) were costly.
- The Commonwealth was critical of Britain's actions in the Suez Crisis.
- South Africa withdrew in 1961 over hostility to its Apartheid regime.
- The Commonwealth leaders were critical of Britain's continuing links with South Africa and its failure to take action when white supremacist Rhodesia declared independence from Britain in 1961.
- Britain's attempt to create new states by amalgamating territories was not always successful, for example in the case of the Central African Federation.
- The Commonwealth disliked attempts to restrict immigration to Britain from 1962.
- The entry into the EEC involved ending preferential treatment for Commonwealth imports, which was resented by countries like New Zealand.

Simple essay style

Below is a sample exam question. Use your knowledge and information on the opposite page to produce a plan for this question. Choose four general points and provide three pieces of specific information to support each general point. Once you have planned your essay, write the introduction and conclusion for the essay. The introduction should list the points to be discussed in the essay. The conclusion should summarise the key points and justify which point was the most important.

Assess the reasons for the decolonisation of Britain's overseas empire between 1951 and 1997.

RAG – Rate the timeline

Below is a sample exam question and a timeline. Read the question, study the timeline and, using three coloured pens, put a red, amber or green star next to the events to show:

- red – events and policies that have no relevance to the question
- amber – events and policies that have some significance to the question
- green – events and policies that are directly relevant to the question.

How well did Britain make the transition from Empire to Commonwealth in the period 1951–97?

1947 India becomes independent
1948 Britain withdraws from Palestine
1950 Korean War
1952 Mau Mau rebellion in Kenya
1954 Britain withdraws from the Sudan
1955 EOKA terrorism in Cyprus to demand independence from Britain
1956 Suez Crisis. British invasion of Egypt condemned
1957 Ghana and Malaysia become independent
1960 'Wind of Change' speech by Macmillan
1960 Cyprus and Nigeria become independent
1961 South Africa leaves Commonwealth
1965 White supremacist regime in Southern Rhodesia declares independence
1968 Britain announced withdrawal 'east of Suez'
1973 Bahamas become independent
1979 Rhodesia settlement – Zimbabwe created
1996 South Africa rejoins Commonwealth
1997 Hong Kong returned to China

Exam focus

Below is a sample exam question and an answer. Read the essay and the comments around it.

How successfully did Britain manage its relations with the USA from 1951 to 1997?

Britain and the USA had been allies during the Second World War and the Cold War had brought them together by Britain receiving Marshall Aid, by their joint co-operation over the Berlin Airlift and by the creation of NATO. With joint military co-operation in the Korean War in 1950, the hope was in 1951 that the Special Relationship would continue to be a cornerstone of British policy. There were times when Anglo–American relations were strong, but this was not true of the whole period. The underlying problem was that the decline of Britain's imperial and military power meant that there was not going to be a relationship on equal terms. This had been obvious as early as 1943. On the whole, though, Britain did manage relations well, though there was some unevenness.

Though not strictly relevant, this sets the scene.

This proposes a point of view which the answer by and large follows.

At the start of the period, the British had demonstrated their solidarity with the USA in opposing the spread of Communism in Asia by their joint action in the Korean War. Asia was a major concern for the USA strategically and Britain and the USA joined in the agreement in Geneva which divided Vietnam in 1954. Britain led one of the most successful anti-Communist military campaigns in Malaya, demonstrating its commitment to suppress Communist-led insurgency, and it also opposed expansion by Indonesia. However, Britain could exert limited influenced over the acceleration of the war in Vietnam by the USA. The ongoing economic problems had led to Britain having limited resources to commit to supporting US actions in Asia. The British withdrawal from its Far East bases in the 1970s left it with limited influence and Britain was unable to broker a peace in Vietnam, while public hostility to the war in the UK made any commitment to support the US impossible while making it difficult to maintain the good relations that existed at the start of the period.

This organises the Asian material into a balanced analysis.

The war had left the USA as an economic and military superpower and able to exert its influence worldwide. The war also meant that it was difficult for Britain to act independently when the USA disapproved. This was shown by the Suez Crisis. The goodwill built up through the Korea situation and the shared stance against Communism did not lead to the USA approving of independent military action by Britain and France since the USA was concerned that the action was likely to drive Nasser into closer relations with the USSR. The British faced an underlying suspicion by the USA that it was pursuing old-fashioned imperialist policy. Eden did not manage relations well over Suez, but the underlying community of interest was strong enough for Macmillan to build fences. There was too little alternative to good relations with the USA; their forces were still in Germany and wartime friendships were still too strong for a permanent breach and British statesmen and diplomats effectively prevented a major breakdown in relations.

This again is balanced but the detail could be stronger.

The strongest ties in the period were probably between Thatcher and Reagan. The Wilson–Heath era had not seen particular warmth, but Thatcher followed Callaghan in establishing good relations. Ideological elements were stronger in ensuring that Thatcher was able to manage relations better than at any time since Churchill. Britain gained considerably from Thatcher's personal diplomacy when the USA offered logistic help with the Falklands War in 1982. Thatcher risked unpopularity by reciprocating in 1986 when American bombers attacked targets in Libya from British bases. But ideology could also divide. Thatcher was concerned that Reagan was not sufficiently committed to maintaining the West's nuclear deterrent in arms limitations talks. Also, her devotion to Britain's imperial past, seen in the Falklands, led to criticism of the US invasion of Grenada in October 1983. Thus there were limits to how much Britain could influence and manage US policy even when personal and political relations seemed strong.

The balanced analysis is better supported here with good examples.

Britain did see the importance of supporting joint action where key interests were involved as when Iraq invaded Kuwait. The commitment of British servicemen, the third largest contingent in the US-led coalition, ensured that Britain showed solidarity and that Britain and the USA acted together in pursuit of common economic and strategic interests in a key region. Whether Britain managed the outcome of the war well is more doubtful, as both Britain and the USA were left attempting to police the Iraqi regime.

Britain did its best to ensure good relations through joint actions in the Gulf War and again in Bosnia, but its ability to influence US policy was more limited and the precedent of supporting US action did lead to unwise intervention in Iraq under Blair, which revealed the problems of Britain being tied to the major guarantor of its security.

Given that Britain did not contribute proportionately to the relationship, it might be seen as an achievement for outwardly strong relations to have been maintained. The USA did not withdraw into isolationism but maintained its presence in Europe during the Cold War era without demanding a huge contribution from Britain. British influence was variable; for example, on Vietnam and also during some key crises like the Cuban Missile Crisis where the USA felt its interests were at stake. Sometimes relations were strained as with Suez and sometimes they seemed somewhat stronger than they were, as in the Thatcher era. The USA supported Britain's closer links with Europe without seeing these as a major challenge to the 'special relationship' and Britain's decolonisation helped to end the US concerns over US resources bolstering the British Empire. Thus, overall, British statesmen managed relations as well as possible given the disparity of resources between the two countries.

> There is a slight drift here into general success of policy and there could have been a rather stronger link back to the question.

> Though outside of the period, there is some balance here.

> The conclusion follows from the analysis and is effective in responding to the question and to the demand for 'assess'.

This is a strong answer which addresses the question directly and has some balance but the level of detailed support could be better. It sets out a clear view at the start and the conclusion follows logically from the analysis.

Exam focus activity

You have now considered four sample high-level essays. Use these essays to make a bullet-pointed list of the characteristics of an A-grade period study essay. Use this list when planning and writing your own practice exam essays.

Glossary

Apartheid A system of racial segregation introduced in South Africa from 1948, designed to preserve the status of the white minority which retained all political power. Races were forbidden to intermarry and were allocated separate residential areas and facilities.

Appeasement Trying to maintain peace by offering concessions and meeting reasonable grievances. It was used specifically to describe the diplomatic efforts of Neville Chamberlain to offer concessions to Hitler to prevent war between 1937 and 1939.

Atlantic Charter A statement of principles agreed by Churchill and Roosevelt in August 1941 affirming common beliefs in freedom and democracy.

Austerity The policy followed by post-war Labour Governments to restrict domestic consumption in order to boost exports and to maintain the balance of payments by import reductions and rationing.

Balance of payments deficit The loss on trade, where imports exceed exports.

Berlin Blockade In 1948 the Soviet Union cut off road and rail access to West Berlin, which was administered by France, Britain and the USA but was within the Soviet-controlled zone of Germany. West Berlin was supplied by air by Britain and the USA from 1948–49 until the Blockade was lifted.

Berlin Wall In 1961 the communist authorities in East Germany built a wall to divide East Berlin from West Berlin to prevent East Germans from fleeing to the West. It stood until 1989.

The Blitz The name given to air attacks on British cities by Germany in the Second World War.

Blitzkrieg 'Lightning war' – a strategy adopted by Germany of air attacks followed by fast-moving armoured vehicles breaking enemy lines.

Bomber Command The branch of the RAF dedicated to bombing offensives.

Butler Act The Education Act of 1944 proposed by R. A. Butler that ensured children would have free secondary education.

Cuban Missile Crisis The USSR backed Castro's Communist regime and in 1962 planned to put nuclear missiles on Cuba. The US President, John F. Kennedy, prevented this with a naval blockade. There was a danger of a full nuclear conflict until compromise was reached and the USSR withdrew,

gaining an agreement by the USA to withdraw its missiles from Turkey.

Czech crisis In response to increasing unrest against communist rule in the 1960s, leader Alexander Dubcek relaxed controls. The USSR sent troops in to overthrow him in 1968.

Devalue (the pound) This means that the official exchange rate for the pound was reduced by the Government making the pound worth fewer dollars, thus making exports cheaper and imports dearer. Unlike today, the governments of the post-war period controlled exchange rates.

Devolution The policy of giving some elements of self government to the different parts of the UK.

Disarmament Reducing weapons and armed forces. The strongest aspect of calls for disarmament after 1945 focused on atomic and nuclear weapons.

Dominions The self-governing parts of the British Empire. For example, Canada, Australia, New Zealand and South Africa.

EEC (European Economic Community) The forerunner of the European Union, where trade between member states had minimal controls while tariffs made goods from non-member states more expensive.

Euroscepticism/Eurosceptics Dislike of many of the aspects of the European Community and distrust of increasing political union

Exchange Rate Mechanism (ERM) Designed to co-ordinate the exchange rates of the different currencies in the EEC.

Falklands War, 1982 When Argentine forces invaded the Falkland Islands, a British colony, in April 1982, Thatcher sent British forces to recapture the islands. Argentina surrendered in June.

Gross Domestic Product (GDP) The annual total value of goods produced and services provided in a country.

General Strike Strikes held by all unions with the object of putting pressure on the government. The only example was in 1926.

Gold Standard The linking of the value of the pound to gold reserves in the bank of England. It was in place before 1914 and then from 1926 to 1931 when it was abandoned.

Hungarian Revolt In 1956 there was a popular revolt against the USSR-installed communist regime in Hungary which was suppressed by

Russian troops. 2,500 Hungarians were killed and 200,000 fled.

Korean War Communist North Korea, backed by Russia and China, invaded non-Communist South Korea in 1950. The war ended when a US-dominated United Nations force (including Britain) drove the Communist forces back to the same position as 1950.

Lease-Lend An agreement with the USA to extend credit for Britain to buy war supplies in the Second World War.

Marshall Aid In 1948, the USA announced a policy of giving aid to war-torn Europe. Offered to all countries, it was rejected by the USSR as a means of increasing Western capitalist influence. In practice it bolstered European countries to prevent economic distress leading to Communism.

Miners' Strike A strike by the coal miners' unions, notably in 1974.

Mods and Rockers Groups whose fights characterised the summer of 1964. 'Mods' rode scooters and were usually more smartly dressed than the 'rockers', who rode motorbikes.

National Government The Government formed in September 1931 by Conservative, Liberal and Labour ministers who joined in a coalition to deal with the severe financial crisis. National Governments were in office 1931–45 but became predominantly Conservative 1935–40.

National Plan An economic strategy in which government would set targets and priorities for economic growth involving control of wages and prices.

Non-Alignment movement A desire by neutral countries to avoid being aligned or associated with either the Communist or the Non Communist blocs supported by Nehru of India and Tito of Yugoslavia.

North Atlantic Treaty Organization (NATO) A Western alliance system began in 1949 and principally supported by the USA to defend its members against aggression. It was obviously directed against the USSR.

Norway Campaign The campaign fought between Germany and Britain to control Norway in 1940, which Britain lost.

Oil crisis of 1973 A big rise in oil prices brought about by the Arab Israeli war.

Poll Tax A tax on the number of adults living in households to replace the traditional local government tax on property (rates). Called the Community Charge, it was nicknamed the Poll Tax after an unpopular tax on heads ('polls') in the fourteenth century.

Rearmament Building up weapons in the 1930s after a period since 1918 when there had been reductions in the armed services.

Real wages Earnings calculated in terms not of money but of what money can actually buy in relation to prices.

Security Council The United Nation's executive body which had five permanent members (the USA, Russia, China, France and the UK) and ten non-permanent members.

Socialism The belief that the power of the state should be used to correct economic injustice and inequalities in society.

'Star Wars' Reagan's Strategic Defence Initiative of developing lasers that could shoot down incoming missiles became known as Star Wars.

Stagflation This combines stagnation and inflation, where industry or the economy declines but prices still rise.

Shareholding The practice of investing in businesses by buying a share of the company which can be bought and sold. Shareholders are paid dividends and according to what sort of shares they hold, and have voting rights about the company's affairs.

Suez Canal A huge canal constructed in 1869 to link the Mediterranean and the Red Sea. It was a major link for Britain to its Asian possessions and to Australia and New Zealand. Its nationalisation by Egypt in 1956 led to an armed expedition by Britain in alliance with France and Israel.

Teddy Boys Youths who dressed in long coats, tight trousers, thick-souled shoes and who had long hair and sideburns seen at the time as 'Edwardian' i.e. like the fashion of the 1900s – hence 'Teddy' boys.

Trench warfare The name given to fighting in the First World War, particularly in France and Belgium, in which both sides dug trenches and fortified them to hold their positions. The land in between became a death trap for attacking forces, and trench warfare led to heavy casualties and limited movement between November 1914 and March 1918.

Welfare state A term meaning that the state takes responsibility for the welfare of its citizens, including their health, housing, environment and employment.

Key Figures

Clement Attlee (1883–1967) Concerned with alleviating poverty in the 1920s and 30s and became Labour leader in 1935. Deputy Prime Minister under Churchill from 1940, he won the 1945 election and presided over radical reforms in the UK and the independence of India. He was leader of the opposition 1951–55.

Tony Blair (b 1953) After being educated at Fettes and Oxford he became a Labour MP who believed in modernising the party, and became leader in 1994. He created 'New Labour' and won the election of 1997 by attracting middle-class support. A master of public relations and communication, he also believed in foreign military interventions and the war in Iraq of 2003 destroyed his reputation.

James Callaghan (1912–2005) After a childhood of poverty he became a civil servant and then joined the navy. A Labour MP since 1945, he went on to be Chancellor of the Exchequer, Home Secretary, Foreign Secretary and, from 1976 to 1979, Prime Minister. He faced union militancy in the Winter of Discontent and was defeated by Thatcher in 1979.

Neville Chamberlain (1869–1940) A distinguished inter-war Conservative Minister of Health, Chancellor of the Exchequer and, from 1937 to 1940, Prime Minister. Best known for his policy of appeasing Nazi Germany, he was later much criticised, but held in the highest esteem by his party and the country for most of his career.

Alec Douglas-Home (1903–95) A junior minister in Chamberlain's Government who supported Appeasement. Foreign Secretary in 1960, he later rejected his peerage and became Prime Minister in 1963 succeeding Macmillan. He was seen as too out of touch with ordinary people, and lost the 1964 election to Harold Wilson.

Anthon Eden (1897–1977) Foreign Secretary in 1935 but resigned in 1938 and had reservations about Appeasement. He was Foreign Secretary again in Churchill's Government in 1940, then later resumed that post in 1951. Long seen as Churchill's successor, he became Prime Minister in 1955 but was discredited by the Suez Crisis and resigned in 1957.

Michael Foot (1913–2010) A fine orator and former radical journalist. He was on the left of the Labour Party, opposing nuclear weapons and calling for more social reforms and nationalisation. He became Labour leader in 1980.

His left-wing opinions and failure to conform in matters of dress lost public approval and divided his party. He resigned after a severe electoral defeat in 1983.

Hugh Gaitskell (1906–63) Minister of Fuel in 1947 and Chancellor of the Exchequer in 1950, during which time he introduced prescription charges. In 1955 he succeeded Atlee as Labour leader. His moderate views were seen as being similar to progressive Toryism and he was criticised by the left of his party. He died unexpectedly in 1963.

Edward Heath (1916–2005) Became leader of the opposition in 1965. He became Prime Minister after the Conservative election victory of 1970, but after calling an election over the Miners' Strike in 1974 he was defeated by Wilson. He was a dedicated European who negotiated British entry into the EEC. He was ousted from the leadership by Margaret Thatcher in 1975.

Neil Kinnock (b 1942) Born into a mining family in South Wales, he became leader of the opposition after Labour's election loss in 1983. He took a firm stance against control by the extreme left of the party but unexpectedly lost the 1992 general election to Major and resigned.

Harold Macmillan (1894–1986) Entered parliament as a Conservative in 1924. He served as the resident Minister in Egypt from 1942–45. He was responsible for an ambitious programme of house-building in 1951–54 and was then Minister of Defence before becoming Chancellor of the Exchequer and then Prime Minster in 1957. He championed the spread of prosperity and also decolonisation in Africa. His later years saw damaging scandals and economic problems, and he resigned in 1963.

Harold Wilson (1916–95) Educated at his local grammar school in Huddersfield, Wilson went on to study and lecture at Oxford. He became a civil servant and entered parliament in 1945, quickly rising to the senior post of President of the Board of Trade in 1947. He resigned over the issue of prescription charges. Shadow Chancellor in 1955 he became Labour Party leader in 1963 and urged modernisation. He won the elections of 1964 and 1966 but was defeated in 1970. He returned as prime minister in 1974 but retired in 1976.

Timeline

1929	Labour wins general election
1931	National Government formed; Churchill is not included
1933	Hitler comes to power in Germany
1935	Government of India Act
1936	Abdication crisis
1938	Hitler annexes Austria ('Anschluss')
1938	Munich crisis
1939	Hitler invades Poland
	Britain declares war on Germany
	Churchill returns to Cabinet
1940	Norway Campaign
	Germany invades Low Countries and France.
	Churchill becomes Prime Minister
	France surrenders
	Battle of Britain
1941	Germany invades USSR
	Atlantic Charter
	USA joins the war
1942	Singapore falls to Japan
	Victory at El Alamein
1943	Britain and USA invade Italy
1944	D-Day landings and campaign in Normandy
1945	Yalta Conference
	Bombing of Dresden
	End of war in Europe
	Potsdam Conference
	Churchill loses general election
	Surrender of Japan
1946	'Iron Curtain' speech
1947	Indian independence; this begins decolonisation
1950	Korean War
1951	Churchill returns as Prime Minister
1953	Iron and steel denationalised
1955	Churchill retires; Eden becomes Prime Minister
1955	Conservatives win general election
1956	Suez Crisis
1957	Macmillan becomes Prime Minister
1958–59	Race riots
1959	Conservatives win general election
1960	Macmillan makes 'Winds of Change' speech
1962	Cuban missile crisis
1963	Profumo scandal
	Douglas-Home becomes Prime Minister
1964	Labour wins general election; Harold Wilson becomes Prime Minister
1965	National Plan
1966	Labour increases majority at general election
1969	'In Place of Strife' published
1970	Conservatives win general election; Heath becomes Prime Minister
1973	Britain joins the EEC
1974	Miners' Strike. Heath loses general election. Wilson becomes Prime Minister again
1975	Referendum on Britain's membership of EEC
1976	Wilson resigns; Callaghan becomes Prime Minister
1979	'Winter of Discontent'
	Conservatives win general election; Thatcher becomes Prime Minister
1982	Falklands War
1983	Conservatives win general election
1984	Miners' Strike
1987	Conservatives win general election
1989	Fall of Berlin Wall
1990	Poll Tax riots
	Britain joins ERM
	Thatcher resigns
	Major becomes Prime Minister
1992	Gulf War
1992	Maastricht Treaty
1992	Conservatives win general election
1997	Labour wins general election; Tony Blair becomes Prime Minister

Answers

Page 9, Spot the inference

Statement 1: X. Cannot be justified from the source. Ponsonby does not represent all of the Labour Party and says favourable things about Churchill.

Statement 2: I. This makes inferences from the source and from the view infers that he was not seen as trustworthy and this did make it difficult for him to be in office.

Statement 3: S. This summarises the source including the points made.

Statement 4: P. This adds a bit to the points made in 3 but is a paraphrase, for example replacing ' a gentleman' with having good manners.

Page 11, Using the provenance

Source A is harsher in tone than B, talking about Gandhiism being crushed and insisting that no agreement should be binding. The emphasis is on maintaining authority. B seems to be more concerned with helping India and showing the benefits of British rule in bringing peace, order and justice. The provenance explains this quite a bit. In 1930, when Churchill was very exercised by the Round Table Conference he was speaking to an audience dedicated to keeping India at all costs and one that agreed with his views. In 1935 he was speaking to the House of Commons which contained many MPs who did not all share his enthusiasm for Empire, so his tone is softer and more persuasive, stressing not sheer authority and the danger from nationalism, but the welfare of Indians. His views have not changed, but the way he expresses them depends on his audience.

Page 13, Doing reliability well

A: Baldwin is justifying why he did not introduce rearmament earlier so he has a **vested interest** in arguing that public opinion would not have accepted it. It may also be that he wants to defend his **reputation**. However, as Prime Minister he would be in a position to know about public opinion, therefore has some **expertise**.

B: Churchill was not in government so he would not be in a position to know about Germany except on the basis of **second hand reports**. This is not to say what he says is not true, but he is reliant on the information of others. It does reflect some **political bias** because he did have a strong belief in defending Britain and its Empire.

C: There is some **political bias** here. Halifax was a minister in a Government which believed in putting economic recovery first and also trying to avoid the costs of rearmament. He was in a position to know, as the Government would have had expert advice on the international situation and all he is saying is that war was not imminent which of course was true given Germany's state of rearmament.

Page 21, Spot the inference

1: X. It cannot be inferred that this is the main reason because it is mentioned first.

2: P. The source is being slightly rewritten.

3: S. Little is being added and the source is being summarised.

4: I. Much more explanation and inference.

Page 23, Doing reliability well

A: Reliable because Wavell was an experienced general and understood military matters but Wavell has a **vested interest** in getting more equipment and may be frustrated at a lack of resources and may be attributing this to Churchill's experience in the Boer War. There is no evidence of such a link given.

B: Reliable because Ismay has direct experience of Churchill's style but possibly unreliable because the source is written with a distinct purpose of keeping Auchinleck motivated and preventing him from taking offence. Churchill may not expect everyone to be equally frank. Reliable because he has enough military experience to know that Churchill's irrelevant memos can be irritating.

C: Reliable because Brooke has first-hand experience and is in a position to know about Churchill. Unreliable because he has an **interest** in being allowed to carry on the war without interference and may be venting frustrations without considering Churchill's reasons for interfering.

D: Unreliable because Churchill is depending on **second-hand information** about the level of preparation and may have a motive to keep Wavell happy in a dangerous situation rather than expressing his true feelings. Also unreliable because he may be more concerned and critical but has a **vested interest** in maintaining morale. Reliable because Churchill was in a position to know as much as possible about what was going on.

Page 27, Explain the differences by using provenance

A shows that Churchill saw the bombing of Germany as justified because Germany had started civilian bombing. It shows a pride in the RAF's achievement of dropping more bombs on Germany than the Germans dropped on Britain and of the scientific and tactical measures.

The speech was a made to London to give confidence that the RAF was retaliating and taking the war directly to Germany and repaying Germany for the damage done to London.

This was at a time when Britain had begun to turn the tide and had driven Germany out of North Africa and also when the Russians were beginning to turn Germany back. However victory was still a long way off and it was important to show what Britain was doing to weaken the German war effort at a time when the cross channel invasion had not yet been launched.

B is showing a much less confident view of bombing and a concern that Britain would be accused of terror for its own sake and also would be left occupying a ruined land, which it would have to sustain and rebuild.

The memo was to senior RAF commanders and was not something that Churchill could admit to in public. It was designed to divert bombing enthusiasts like Arthur Harris from excessive destruction now that Britain was closer to victory and to restore political considerations of reputation over military concerns.

By 1945 it was clear that victory was closer, that soon Britain would have to be planning a post-war world so the tone is very different from the source produced in 1943 when victory was still far off.

Page 29, Add your own knowledge

Agreement: In A, Churchill refrains from making promises about the future. This links with B's view that he was wrong for the reconstruction of England and C as people were disgruntled by the housing shortage – something Churchill was not willing to make promises about. These agree that it was his fault, confirmed by B's view of his talking 'rot' about the Gestapo.

Differences: C praises Churchill's speech while B says it was 'rot'. C blames Labour propaganda but B blames Churchill. A supports C in that Churchill is trying to avoid raining false hopes and therefore is responsible in his attitude rather than being to blame.

Knowledge: A – Churchill was in office in 1918–20 and saw the damage that unfulfilled promises did but 'airy visions of Utopia' dismisses genuine hopes for a fairer society raised by responsible wartime reports like Beveridge. B – Churchill thought that the degree of state control promised by Labour would involve some sort of Gestapo to enforce. As B says this was unrealistic.

The Labour leaders were moderates who had shared power with Churchill and there was enough support for reform not to need enforcement by the police. C mentions the important service vote. There was more political awareness and hopes for both peace and social change among the armed forces and some fear that Churchill would engage in war against Russia.

Page 35, Spot the inference

Statement 1: Inference – the view is explained.

Statement 2: Summary

Statement 3: Paraphrase

Statement 4: There is no evidence for this view in the source.

Page 41, Explain the differences by using provenance

A: Europe has undergone a tragedy and needs to become a family. The Swiss model of co-operation is put forward for Europe as a whole i.e. a federal model like the USA – a common political union and common citizenship.

It was made to a Swiss university audience and reflected the need in 1946 for Europe to be united to prevent another war.

Churchill was not in office so he could afford to offer grand solutions without considering the practicalities of making such a union.

B: This is a view that European unity is not really important. It says that neither Britain nor the Commonwealth should ever become part of any such European union or federal structure. Not Europe but the Empire and Commonwealth should be Britain's priority.

It was not a grand speech made in public but it was to the Cabinet on Churchill's return to power to set out what policy should be.

Churchill was back in office. He knew that it would be hard to negotiate a European union on the basis of his idealistic Zurich speech as Britain relied on the USA for defence and for the Empire and Commonwealth for much of its economy.

Page 51, Spot the mistake

There is no accurate reference to social change but rather political and economic matters.

Page 53, Support or challenge?

Statement 1: support; 2: support; 3: challenge; 4: support; 5: support; 6: support; 7: challenge; 8: support.

55, Delete as applicable

Most would argue that he was the most successful leader to a **great** extent and was a **skilled** communicator. He was more able than **all** the others and was **a great deal** more prepared to make changes.

Page 61, Eliminate irrelevance

The section on Wilson's premiership ('Wilson's premiership did not always put into practice what the Prime Minister had promised and he found that economic problems were often too difficult to allow reforms') is not relevant – this is not a reason for his 1964 victory. Nor is the last sentence relevant.

Page 65, Complete the paragraph

On balance, the most important reason is not so much Heath's strengths but the economic situation which seemed to be out of control and which was blamed on Labour leadership. (This is an example of a clear judgement not a definitive answer.)

Page 67, The flaw in the argument

The flaw is that too much is weighted towards explaining the election result and there is not enough about what was actually achieved in terms of fulfilling Heath's aims. The answer could be improved by going back to what Heath wanted to do and showing how much he was able to put into practice.

Page 69, Spot the mistake

The main factor is referred to but then the paragraph moves away from this point. The paragraph needs to make the factor of industrial relations central and give it more attention and deal with why it is more important than other factors.

Page 73, Develop the detail

There needs to be more detail with regard to which Labour leaders and why did they not appeal to the public; for example, Michael Foot had a poor public image and policies of nationalisation seemed old fashioned. More detail should be added to the issues that Labour were divided over – for example, nuclear policy. Which Labour manifestos were unpopular and which one in particular was considered a 'suicide note' (1983)?

Page 75, Turning assertion into argument

Thatcher's policies fell heavily on the working class and this cannot be seen as a success. Unemployment remained rather high and was particularly severe in areas of heavy industry.

Thatcher successfully encouraged more enterprise by reducing taxation and deregulating financial services.

Thatcher successfully dealt with inflation which had been high in the 1970s but fell thanks to deflationary budgets, for example in 1980 and 1981.

Page 77, Complete the paragraph

The consequences of social change were seen more clearly in some areas, particularly in the industrial regions and in London, but major consequence was the increasing gap between rich and poor.

Page 79, Introducing an argument

The introduction should offer more judgement about the reasons. For example:

The main one was because the revolutionary changes had been made and the Thatcher government was beginning to show signs of not dealing with economic problems. This more than Thatcher's personality was the key factor.

The conclusion needs a judgement, too. For example:

By 1990 there were serious issues which many felt could not be dealt with by Thatcher's assertive and dynamic style. However, it was not her personality that was the main reason for her fall …

Page 81, Develop the detail

The paragraph could be more detailed by referring to Blair and what he offered. The issue over Europe could be developed. Also, some Eurosceptics could be mentioned and their other views explored. Why Labour seemed more modern could be explained.

Page 85, Develop the detail

When Stalin died in 1953 and Khrushchev took over there were expectations of a thaw because of internal changes. The events in Hungary in 1956 when Soviet forces invaded the country to suppress anti-Communist opposition could be explained. Also, the events of 1968 and the Prague Spring could be referred to. The British public were shocked to see Soviet tanks in Prague.

Page 89, Eliminate irrelevance

The first two sentences are not about opposition and neither is the last sentence.

Page 91, Identify an argument

The second sample tries to assess the reasons, arguing that one factor is more important, but the first sample merely explains them.

Page 93, You're the examiner

This is a middle band answer because it outlines well why the crisis was serious but has little about whether it was the most serious, except for a final assertion.

Page 95, Rate the timeline

1947: green; 1948: red; 1950 red; 1952: green; 1954: amber; 1955: green; 1956: red; 1957: green; 1960: (1) green, 1960 (2) green; 1961: amber; 1965: amber; 1968: amber; 1973: green; 1973: green; 1996: amber; 1997: red.